REVOLUTION
AMERICA

Communication Toolbox For The Modern
Conservative American Woman

by

Erin Cruz

MOtivational PRESS®
LEADERS IN GLOBAL PUBLISHING

Published by Motivational Press, Inc.
1777 Aurora Road
Melbourne, Florida, 32935
www.MotivationalPress.com

Manufactured in the United States of America.

ISBN: 978-1-62865-487-5

CONTENTS

DEDICATION

To my late husband Rene Leonardo Cruz. In my life there have been many greats. Great faith. Great family. Great loves. Great friends. All of these lead to great experiences and great memories. Of those greats, there is one truly great man who challenged me through the best and worst. He inspired me in everything, pushing me with patience and positivity. His greatness was unsurpassed, really. You see, to everyone else he was addressed or introduced as Professor, PhD, expert, internationally renowned, a scholar, a creator, a pioneer in his field, but to me, he was my husband and my love. I called him "baby" and he called me "love."

When we met, this great man was on the polar opposite spectrum politically from where I stood. Our political leanings were not in sync at all. There were never debates on issues. In our home there was only room for proper discourse. We had something in common though which brought us together. We love truth. If one can accept truths, one can find common ground. Common ground is something that is needed today, desperately.

This man, he taught me so many things, one of which was to always ask the question, "Why?" This word "why" is the collector of truth and without it we often, as a people, will have nothing much to talk about or rally around on any level or in any common experience. "Three letters," he would say, "have more power to change than any complex question you could ask."

This man wanted me to be involved in my community. He wanted me to start writing books much sooner than I did. It wasn't that I couldn't it was only that I spent my time journaling, note taking, observing, and interacting. I would jot ideas down as they came, observations as I experienced them. He would say, "Why do you write information down if you aim to do nothing with it?" He was right.

It is because of him, how great he was, that I am who I am today. It is because of him that I asked so many times that simple question, "Why?" It is because of him, I have a book to dedicate. I am forever and eternally grateful for this great man who was my friend, my family, and my love. Dedicating the creative knowledge I have attained since 1999 is not only an honor it is a privilege.

This is for you, baby.

ACKNOWLEDGEMENT

FOR ALL OF THE MANY times people have asked, "What are you thinking about?" I have to say thank you. Thank you for your understanding, guidance, and encouragement. Every one of you were so patient when I responded with the words, "nothing," "this and that," "writing in my head," all of the way to the response, "just a minute, let me write this down." You have all been blessed with more patience than Job.

I give thanks to God for inspiring me, to my late husband who taught me, and life, which grew me. I am grateful for encouragers and motivators in my family and friend circles, my mother and father, my children, specifically. To those who saw me frustrated and know that I have so many works in progress yet you all are continually rooting me on, offering your perspective and individual knowledge and insight. You are Godsends.

My best friend, you know who you are. Your love and support has been immeasurable, thank you. We may not always agree on the issues but you have been honest in your feedback. You, my dear, are the best friend this Modern Conservative American Woman could have.

A special thank you to my Manager, Rob Lowe and Brinka Lowe at Casting New Lives for pairing me up with the dynamic team at Motivational Press, and Justin Sachs. This wouldn't be possible without you seeing the vision Rene did and pushing me to step forward in my gifts. I am forever grateful to all of you.

To my mentors, colleagues, special patriots that have helped me through the years, you know who you are, thank you. Specifically, Natalie Neal Whited, your guidance and helping me polish a knowledgebase that supported ten years of growth thus far is being put to good use. You are a masterpiece and a national treasure.

A truly special thank you to Lieutenant Colonel Jeffrey L. Clark, USA. You, sir, have helped to keep me focused and motivated through this process. Reminding me always that a fit mind and body will accomplish many things. A true patriot and man of God, thank you.

To the countless fellow Patriots throughout the nation who I speak to everyday, you are the reason I wrote this book. Thank you for your continued support of the Republic and remaining determined to see her strong, uniting even among the divide. God Bless you and God Bless America.

PROLOGUE

THE YEAR IS 1999. My children are small. There is little time to make dinner and do homework after working full time with a commute. Add on to that, I was a single mother at the time. Politics, there really isn't a place, or really a space in my life for such things. Where is the time? Life was moving by quickly.

September 11, 2001. I am in my kitchen. The children are still in bed. It is too early to think clearly when I get a phone call from my mother. It is happening. My mother is watching a terrorist attack play out on United States soil. The news, my mother's voice was so disturbing to me, what she was telling me, the description of what was happening, it didn't register in my mind in entirety. I felt helpless.

I couldn't turn on a TV to watch what she was seeing. We were poor and didn't have cable at the time. I stood there listening as my mother's voice shook as she told me what she was watching on the TV. The reality was the children and I lived in downtown San Diego and all of the money we had went to sending my kids to private school which was right next to our World Trade Center in San Diego. I lived not too far away. Would downtown San Diego be next? No one knew what exactly would play out that morning. So many lives were devastated by the 9/11 terrorist attacks, as Americans our family was grieving the loss as well.

I kept the children home. We drove up to the country where my family lived. This was the first time since Ronald Reagan I had paid any real attention to politics. Given my age, Ronald Regan was a childhood dreamboat presidency, saving us from recession and financial disaster. That was my memory of Regan way back.

Terror pushed me into politics the first time and the second was a much larger but different threat. Now mark my view, many see him as a hero. Personally this is not the case for me. Barack Hussein Obama, a junior, not even one term Senator from Illinois was to run for President of the United States of America. It is now 2007. There are so many questions to be answered. Who is this guy? Where did he come from? Does he mean what he is saying? People couldn't agree on much of anything after all of the turmoil of the prior president and the divide that had begun, economically and then socially. This was compounded seven years to follow.

Like in 2016, in 2007 and 2008, so many people wanted something different. With the Housing Crisis now in full loom and collapse somewhat in sight, Barack Obama is elected. Hope and Change is what the people voted for. Not me of course, but many did. And then we, those who were opposed to the Obama Presidency saw it clear as day. There was an agenda. A full push toward the separation and segregation of women and men as the gender base, subsets of gender were introduced. A number of initiatives were ushered in which aimed at the breakdown of traditional and conservative values. At the core or bulls eye of the aim was our healthcare system, though that was just one point there was a much bigger picture in mind. That picture was to tear the fabric of our nation by dividing us so far apart congress could do as they please.

Not many recognize this but the strategy was paid for, well outlined, and many years later would be exposed. Patriots coined the term "Grubbered." As in, the American people were Grubbered. The term was named after the man responsible for the manufacturing of financial and social platforms outlining the plan for selling and administering Health Care Reform, or ObamaCare across the United States.

Really, the divisive plan was to divide the people and cause so much ruckus no one would see what was happening. You see the biggest divide came right here, defining what Health Care Reform should look like. This action brought out nearly ever base of division that could be waged to divide the American people. Marriage and LGBTQ issues, abortion, right to life, socio economic divide with Medicaid, entitlement arguments that were knowingly mislabeled for agenda, the list goes on. Of course we know Health Care Reform was just one piece of the bigger pie.

This breakdown, the polarizing of the sacred dinner table by the White House insisting we discuss ObamaCare over Thanksgiving dinner, the passing of Health Care Reform on Christmas Eve while we were all busy with family, this agitating was the start of Revolution America. It was unavoidable really.

Add to this, families losing their homes, fear over government overreach into our healthcare system, into our health care itself. Separating Doctor from patient. People were desperate to keep their freedoms and communicate their values and need for independence from government. The marches began. The divide continued.

As we see, Revolution America, the coming together of the mind within each home must be attained. It won't come without struggle. The conversations can get tense. Presidents have changed hands and there most certainly are still so many issues unresolved. Hope and Change ushered in a new level of divide, one that is reaching into homes across America and the world.

This is where I believe we can make an impact. It seems distant, but it is possible to attain. Where there are issues or problems there must be solutions. The challenge comes in determining the best form of communication to accomplish ones desired outcome. How do we figure out what that conversation looks like? Through looking at the lives of Modern Conservative Women and several older and newer forms of communication techniques we will aim to close the gap within our own lives and reach out to our communities. This is your own personal Revolution America, one person, one conversation at a time.

FOREWORD

THE TWENTY-FIRST CENTURY has seen the explosion of public interaction and participation in the political arena beyond what most Americans and political observers could have ever predicted. The polarization of political views from progressive to conservative has escalated like a meteor approaching an object: seen but not anticipated to arrive at such a speed of light pace. The added emphasis of making each and every issue a personal one has also placed a unique focus on the role and importance of considering the impact upon the participation and support of the woman as a citizen and voter. While not overly surprising, this phenomena has brought new meaning and importance to reaching the politically active in all generations and demographic backgrounds. Nearly a decade ago, Erin Cruz was on the sidelines, watching and wondering what was going on in American Politics. Today she is in the middle of the game, prodding and pushing all those around her to be engaged and meaningful, to go forward toward your, and her, destiny. Erin has labeled this change as the "Revolution" in American politics.

This "Revolution" of freeing up and expanding participation, especially by the women of America, has thrown many, if not most political activists and pollsters into a "heads over heals" rethinking of how to brand and market issues and candidates. Not just by labels such as "Conservative" or "Liberal" or "Progressive" but by values and principles and economic strata are the lobbyists and party leaders now looking at what makes women get involved and become leaders at various points. The labeling of the people getting more involved has been both a changing dogma but also one where no one label seems to fit most women in the political arena these days.

From many viewpoints, the typical is no longer a valid description. To see the impassioned explosion of activism at all levels has been extraordinary. To find examples and live action candidates is special and now more important with the recent change in representation of our federal and many locally elected leaders in 2016. Erin Cruz is one of these examples and her perspectives are thought provoking. As the leadership author Stephen R. Covey coined in the early 2000's, "All people have a need to live, to love, to learn, and to leave a legacy." This may be one of the moving factors that makes "Revolution America" an important read for women and men to sense the change that is impacting our entire generation and representative republic. Who are we; what skills and techniques do we need to participate? Since this is a fast moving and not completely understood change, read on and get ready to have an "A Ticket Ride" to the next level, wherever you believe that politics in America may be headed.

Justin Sachs, Best-Selling Author of 8 books on
*Business and Leadership including the **Power of Persistence***

Chapter One

FIRE IN MY BELLY

IT IS 2008 AND THE PRESIDENTIAL Election seems to be flying by. Tensions are high. As a conservative, there are too many questions unanswered about one of the men running for office: Barack Hussein Obama. Unfortunately, every conversation I have about the election leaves blood at full boil on both sides of the conversation. Full boil is happening regardless of the political party of the person I am talking to is a part of. Can this really be the case? How is it that we, as Americans, let things get so bad we cannot even have a civil conversation? How is it that we, as conservative women and leaders in our homes, have allowed such a thing to happen in our midst?

Frustration, agitation, and many other things led to the marching of my fingers to the internet for answers. There is little to be learned on the Internet, but there is an unlimited expanse that can be learned by connecting to others. I will give you some insight as to how I see our movement as Modern Conservative American Women and what and how we can approach taking action. I have learned a great deal over the last nine years. I really have a burning in my belly to share with you my knowledge so you don't have to tread so heavily through the deep in and outs—you can jump right in and take action.

First, lets fast-forward and look at today. Today's conservative American woman leads the revolution of modern conservatism on multiple fronts and is faced with situational dynamics that are unprecedented. The current divided political climate in America demands a savvy, soft, and pliable approach by the conservative woman in every facet of her life. We call her a Modern Conservative American Woman, leader in the restoration of American values. I will share with you later the differences between Modern Conservative American Women and other forms of Women as I see them, from the real world—not from a dictionary.

First, before we go further, let me introduce myself. I am Erin Cruz. I am a petite but fierce constitutional conservative political activist, mother, and friend to nearly all I meet, and as I see it, I have mastered the art of political understanding and conversation. I will be sharing many of my experiences and hopefully shine a light on some areas of communication, providing tools to help you more effectively communicate the conservative cause across party lines and really, with people in general. Political party should be limited and not highlighted in much communication because really, it takes away from the fundamental communication of people at the human level. We really need to get back to the basics folks, and we will. I will touch on my interaction with both Democrats and Republicans, from far left progressives and liberals to the more conservative Democrat all the way through to the rightest leaning right or alt-right conservative, the conservatarian or conservative libertarian, constitutional conservative as well as the moderate conservative on various topics such as healthcare, abortion, racism, LGBT, and various activist topics. As a whole, though, we all want the same things and I think understanding this will help communicate across the party divide, on that human level. I will share with you so many insights from my journey. There are some exciting and effective techniques I have used to communicate both values and principles while being able to keep the conversation going. Shocker, right?! After Election 2008 and Election 2012 I was not sure this would be possible.

Rewind again. Don't get whiplash! It was after the 2008 election was concluded that I started to discover a trend. Back in 2009 I saw a major divide in the nation around policies affecting families of all backgrounds, driving women to the front of the fight for their families, their health care needs, and at the core, the fight for retention of freedom from government overreach. This was a non-partisan divide over party lines, if that makes any sense. And, yes, women, conservative women in particular were (and still are) front and center once again.

It was then that I made a decision to start a conversation with other conservatives across social media and found this fight was not my own. By joining the Tea Party, Tea Party Patriots, Smart Girl Politics, among another half a dozen or more groups and pairing it with social media I was now enlightened to see the conversations being had not just on one side, on both sides. I learned the conversation people were having was all wrong and non productive. People across the nation were more divided than ever, even more so than I originally thought. Political conversations on all fronts were at times hostile, tense, heated, causing fractions in relationships all around me. It was shocking to say the least. The divide was driving to the center of the family unit, of which women are front and center. I know I mention this a great deal, but it needs to be realized.

So I set off, with that fire in my belly and over the last five years I have had the opportunity to work and find the fine line and medium where people from all backgrounds can come together. Some encounters have been unfruitful, many people do not want to compromise, understand, or change their point of view. That is ok. Lesson learned: move on. One common thing I found centric to the majority of people and it narrowed my conversation to just this, the family unit. At their core, people want a sound and fulfilling life. They want good things for themselves and their family. They want to be happy.

By touching on the basic desire of people while applying certain techniques of conversation and tailoring ones approach to the individual, I found that whether you are talking to your mother, child, co-worker, someone in the grocery store, and even if the conversation gets tense, perhaps hostile, neutralization is almost always possible. Like most families or social groups, there is that "one" person who just can't get along, upsetting the entire event over political or social differences, it is possible to further the conservative cause, without following the misconception of silence being the best policy. Yes, It is possible.

Silence is not always the best policy. It is how you are silent that carries weight. Women being at the forefront of the Conservative Revolution are pressed from all angles on how to nurture, maintain, and grow all types of relationships; silence will not accomplish or further the cause. What is needed to be exercised by today's modern woman is Resolve. There in lies the key to achieving the goals needed to further all relationships. We can discover Resolve by looking at the role of other Conservative women in recent United States history. We will touch on the lives of three conservative, better yet, conservatarian women: Jeanette Rankin, Ginger Rogers, and Zora Neale Hurston. Yes, Ginger Rogers was a Conservative Republican woman. Also looked at later on in the book is the life of a Conservative Revolutionary from the United Kingdom, Margaret Thatcher. The fire in my belly led me to think about different women in history I had learned about and witnessed in my childhood and early adult years. We will take a look at their personal as well as professional lives, how they interacted with both family and peers within their profession, and their impact on conservatism as a whole. You and I may not agree with all aspects, but surely my observations will prove to be interesting and shed some light on even not so modern, modern day Resolve.

As we peek through the Resolve and forms of communication in the real world of modern day politics, I would like to share some methods that have changed the way I look at and approach communication. Though they seem basic, and somewhat laughable, the terms used in The Tool Box are highly effective and easy to remember. We will use some old acronyms and introduce you to some new ones, not just to get your communication skills going, but also to help you gain new perspective on how to better communicate while keeping things light. You may be familiar with communication acronyms SOLER or SURETY, if not, you will learn about them.

One thing is for sure, when under pressure it is difficult to remember long acronyms. Me, I like simple and easy to remember things, every day things that will work in real life, in the real world. I have a funny story I will share with you about the one night where theses acronyms woke me up, literally.

Life has taught me enlightenment doesn't come on its own out of thin air. I firmly believe enlightenment comes with knowledge. From examining the history of the conservative woman from household to the political playground, as well as picking apart known and proven communication techniques used in various fields, while adding in easy to remember tools to communicate, we as women, from a feminine and strong perspective, will be empowered and thus enlightened to communicate more effectively. The gents may also benefit from this as well, so share away. The more people who tap into their life actions and re-think their thinking and fill up their Tool Kit, the better.

Now more than ever, it is important that we foster inclusion, love, prosperity, trust, and stay true to the values we hold. Alienating those around us, whether we agree with their values or their views, will not assist us in attaining the goals at the core of the conservative movement. My hope is that by using the techniques I share with you, you will be able to communicate more clearly and help nurture relationships within your family, within your workplace, and within your peer groups. The fire in my belly has inspired and pushed me for nearly a decade to discover a better way to reach those we love and steer our nation in the direction that nurtures the American Dream, burning within, finally it is let out to communicate to you and others like you what I have learned with the intention of you growing your own love for this great nation and reaching beyond, into your own family and circle of love and freedom.

Chapter Two

DISCOURSE IN DISGUISE

A MERICA HAS SHIFTED. The social structures, the manner in which Americans communicate, all have moved to a more coarse and tense beast of sorts. I would like to take you on a mini journey to look at a few topics, words we will look at as they relate to how we communicate, in modern day America, though it more than likely is also seen within other westernized nations as well.

Roll back about twenty-five to thirty years to the late 1980's and early 1990's. Back to what at the time many saw as wild and provocative. In the music industry, there were the crazy lace gloves of Madonna and the bright red jackets of Michael Jackson, and then there was the wild hair of Billy Idol, and even a touch of psychedelic black and white makeup of the group known as Metallica. The days where the music industry started putting forth music videos kids all around the country would flock to see on the television. The time shift also saw one of its most conservative hay days under Ronald Regain and seeing the Iron Curtain fall and the free world find a little more peace. When families would gather, most times we could all talk some politics without Uncle Joe absolutely losing it and Cousin Tammy getting so upset she has to leave the room. The children looking on in either confusion or simply left with memories, which shape their view not only toward family, but also about the topics overheard. Children are our future and must be considered a priority any time we interact, especially about hot topics. Woman in particular are impacted a great deal in this regard as they are most often times the ones leading the communication as it relates to the children and the mood which the home front carries forward throughout the day.

The climate has changed in the way we communicate around politics as well as hot topic issues of the day. Something most people, regardless of political affiliation can recognize on the surface. But what does this mean, exactly? We will go in to the matter and relation of the word "discourse" at length. It isn't always apparent that the hot topics being discussed are matters, political in nature, and certainly, many times, it isn't apparent there is disagreement or debate at all, until it is seemingly too late. Mainly, the discussion should be dealt with using mutual respect, the topics of discussion should be approached with the amount of respect that both parties offer one another, and that proper discourse is deserving of.

Hopefully, applying the techniques used in Revolution America we will together be able to manifest the types of values we hold true to our family and be a living example to the outside world, fostering the change we desperately need to restore the American family.

So lets take a look at "discourse." The word as I see it is not given enough weight in modern times. Discourse is a word that should be thought of in terms of balance. Instead, it appears that it has a different meaning or implied usage from generation to generation. In my humble opinion it needs a come back!

To look at the usage of the word in the real world of modern times I approached two age groups about the word. The ages were over twenty-one through the age of thirty and the second group was forty and older. The responses were polar opposite.

First, I asked twenty people under 40 years old what this word means and/or what it means to them. Only three of twenty knew what the word meant and how it is active in every day life. Pretty frightening. In stark contrast, I asked twenty people over the age of 50 the same question and only a mere two individuals were unsuccessful at attaining the true meaning and usage of the word.

This tells us a few things. First, there appeared to be a loss in the power and value of a word in the younger generation and that interaction in real life lends it to be more casual for this age group. Also, it shows based on their responses that interactions are more emotionally based. In the older generation, there appeared to be a desire to take a moment and clearly communicate their responses to me. This was not only evident in how they defined the word off of the top of their heads, but also that their words in their response as well as the word "discourse" clearly held value and meaning to them. In the response of the over 50 crowd it also was apparent their responses, though still leaning towards fairly casual, were spoken with authority and purpose. I didn't find in my interviews that there was a large disparity as it related to gender. There was more of an age gap that bounced out at the gender angle and showed the clearer divide being age. Interesting for sure.

To the definition as stated online in Merriam-Webster:

Definition of *discourse[1]*

Discourse:

1 *archaic*: the capacity of orderly thought or procedure: rationality

2 : verbal interchange of ideas; *especially*: conversation

Even when looking at the definition in its most basic form we can clearly see balance is at the center of this word. The definition in both one and two talk about "orderly thought," "rationality," "interchange of ideas," and "conversation." Right away you can get a feel for this word. It has presence to it. There is substance and balance that is irrefutable. Once more I see there really is no other way to accept this word can be interpreted differently, only in that it might have been passed down to the younger generation as a derogatory word. With that said, I find it important we correct this in our own worlds and circles and make this word a "tick" word that we can make stick.

The words that I believe more accurately describe the communication taking place in Modern American society today is "dispute." Another word that is being played out, inappropriately in my opinion, within our homes is "debate." If we take a look at both of those words, it is clear that "discourse" is being used where these two words are taking action in our homes and within our society.

Definition of *dispute[2] and debate[3]*

Dispute:

intransitive verb

:to engage in argument: debate; *especially*: to argue irritably or with irritating persistence

transitive verb

1   *a* : to make the subject of verbal controversy or disputation *Legislators hotly disputed the bill.*

2   *b*: to call into question or cast doubt upon *Her honesty was never disputed. The witness disputed the defendant's claim.*

2   *a*: to struggle against: oppose *disputed the advance of the invaders b*: to contend over *disputing ownership of the land*

Debate:

intransitive verb

1   obsolete: fight, contend

2   *a*: to contend in words

b: to discuss a question by considering opposed arguments

3   to participate in a debate *the six primary candidates who debated last night*

transitive verb

1   *a*: to argue about *the subject was hotly debated*

b: to engage (an opponent) in debate *a governor debating her challenger*

2   to turn over in one's mind: to think about (something, such as different options) in order to decide *still debating what to do*

When Aunt Jane is attempting to tell Cousin Mitch something about the current election cycle and she is getting completely heated trying to communicate a point her conversation likely shifts from what could be constructive discourse to a debate or even a dispute. At first glance, Auntie Jane tries to sound conversational, even kind but when someone such as Cousin Mitch leans in, either asking questions or trying to prove his point she and many like her, instead of sticking with polite discourse, squeamishly shies away or too easily gets upset. In turn this shifts the conversation.

So, what made or instigated this shift? Was it body language? Was it perhaps the shift in Auntie's voice, or her facial expressions? It lends one to wonder, could it have been because Cousin Mitch had a shift in body language, tone of voice, or facial expression? It could have been both Auntie Jane and Cousin Mitch couldn't it!

It is quite safe to say there is a high likelihood it was as a result of multiple factors, points of the topic matter they were discussing, voice inflections, facial micro-expressions, and body language. The only sure fire way to know is if you witnessed the conversation yourself.

Communication is highly complex, but if you can learn even just a hint of what to look for and learn to be *responsive* rather than *reactionary* you will become a better communicator in no time. Later on as we get into the Tool Box we will look at different forms of communication more in depth and what might be good responses as opposed to reactions in varying situations.

As women, we especially can benefit from learning how to master our response. Though research has shown that women are in general hold a larger role in communication and in many ways overpower their male counterparts where this is concerned. Though as a whole this can also contribute to other weaker forms of communication exchanges, so if we can fully master our ability as women to be more expressive, and can absorb techniques that can assist us in mastering our outward communication not only will we be better off, our communication will benefit and our families and many other aspects of our life will flourish as well.

Chapter Three

MODERN CONSERVATIVE AMERICAN WOMAN

I HAVE HEARD THIS over and over, "Erin, you are sexist." Laughter, belly laughter comes right out of me. It just happens and I can't help but laugh. It also shows how narrow-minded people can actually be. And they don't mean it in a good way, and they say this. "Erin, you are sexist, and not in a good way!" I always ask why they say this. I will mention most people are surprised by my answer, "Well, no. I am not sexist." People really struggle with the idea that I believe that people are created equal. Yes, they are. While people are equal, in general, men and women are not the same. Unfortunately many people who enter this conversation with me struggle so much to try to wrap their minds around the concept and their entire lives where they learned one thing at home, another thing in their private lives, and another at school, and yet another in the books they read, apparently the reconciliation of all areas doesn't compute when confronted with my perspective. It is highly unfortunate. Truly a loss.

I say, THINK for yourself. Really think about your life and what has worked, what hasn't. What has ironed out and what you can't buy a large enough can of starch to iron out. You know, as I tell some folks, at times you need to just burn what isn't working and start over. Throw out what is not serving you anymore in the ways of thinking. What use is your current way of thinking if the results produced are substandard and not allowing your life to flourish?

When I look at the American lifestyle I grew up in, not much compares. It is what we do with it that matters most, like many things. As it pertains to the Modern American Woman, I see several aspects that we as Conservatives can highlight to help substantiate our role, as the Modern Conservative American Woman to help further our great nation in every aspect of our lives.

First, lets look at terms in general as we did earlier with some words and terms. We have the general view of certain terms. Who defines them? We know there is a specific definition of words, yes. That does not mean we as a group or collection of women can't define our own group. Indeed, we cannot allow the Left or liberals to define our world. There is no reason we as Modern Conservative American Women can't define our own roles in society ourselves. I see it as a must that we assert our roles, not only within the familial unit, but within society as a whole. It is high time we stop allowing others, especially in media or other more left leaning areas, say what we are or what we are not. So, with that in mind, here are the general categories I see as women in Modern American History, by all means this is not the full list, only a small segment of important categories I will address:

Woman

Traditional Woman

Modern Woman

Feminist Woman

Conservative Woman

Liberal Woman

American Woman

Take a look. Think on these few terms for 5 minutes. Which encompasses you or your wife or your mother, girlfriend, sister, friend, daughter, aunt, and so on. It is important to think about this.

In several areas throughout the text you will find I repeat myself. This is for good reason. The more you think on the areas of discussion the more your mind will have to process in different ways, either the words, the techniques, or the areas of focus. This all will play a roll not only in learning but really seeking out in your specific mind the areas that are weak or that need strengthening within your life. It is a good thing. So re-read the list above one more time. Lets go through the definitions now:

Woman[4]:

1   a: an adult female person

b: a woman belonging to a particular category (as by birth, residence, membership, or occupation) —usually used in combination *councilwoman*

2:   womankind[5]: [female human beings : women especially as distinguished from men]

3: distinctively feminine nature : womanliness

Traditional (adj)[6] [Woman]

1   a: an inherited, established, or customary pattern of thought, action, or behavior (such as a religious practice or a social custom)

b: a belief or story or a body of beliefs or stories relating to the past that are commonly accepted as historical though not verifiable

2   the handing down of information, beliefs, and customs by word of mouth or by example from one generation to another without written instruction

3   cultural continuity in social attitudes, customs, and institutions

-- *Traditional* \-'dish-nəl, -'di-shə-nᵊl\ *adjective*

Modern[7] [Woman]

1 a: of, relating to, or characteristic of the present or the immediate past: contemporary *the modern American family*

b: of, relating to, or characteristic of a period extending from a relevant remote past to the present time *modern history*

2   involving recent techniques, methods, or ideas: up-to-date *modern methods of communication*

3   *capitalized*: of, relating to, or having the characteristics of the present or most recent period of development of a language *Modern English*

Feminist (n or adj)[8] [Woman]

1   the theory of the political, economic, and social equality of the sexes

2   organized activity on behalf of women's rights and interests

-- feminist \'fe-mə-nist\ *noun or adjective*

Conservative (n)[9] [Woman]

1   *a*: an adherent or advocate of political conservatism

b capitalized: a member or supporter of a conservative political party

2   *a*: one who adheres to traditional methods or views

b: a cautious or discreet person

Liberal (n)[10] [Woman]

1   *a*: of, relating to, or based on the liberal arts *liberal education*

b archaic: of or befitting a man of free birth

2   *a*: marked by generosity: openhanded *a liberal giver*

b: given or provided in a generous and openhanded way *a liberal mealc*: ample, full

3   *obsolete*: lacking moral restraint: licentious

4   not literal or strict: loose *a liberal translation*

5   broad-minded; *especially* : not bound by authoritarianism, orthodoxy, or traditional forms

6   *a*: of, favoring, or based upon the principles of liberalism

b capitalized: of or constituting a political party advocating or associated with the principles of political liberalism; *especially* : of or constituting a political party in the United Kingdom associated with ideals of individual especially economic freedom, greater individual participation in government, and constitutional, political, and administrative reforms designed to secure these objectives

American [Woman]

3 a native or inhabitant of the U.S. : a U.S. citizen

Now, lets go through the vision of what and how I see and view these definitions enacted in the "real" world. In your case, you and I may differ in our interpretation of each term. Please hold on to the perspective that while we may differ on these points there is a reason behind why I define the groupings in the way I do.

As you follow through the text, if your opinions differ from my own, actively compare in your mind those differences with how I present the material. In doing so, you will learn more about your views from the beneficial part of your mind and life perspective that expresses empathy, approaching contrary lines of thought that challenge your own. This will benefit your world areas that impact you every day, in situations later that you never may have recognized until visiting this mode of learning and perspective, especially on this topic.

There also may be a point in the book, in which you don't understand what I am talking about. Keep going. Only, go ahead and highlight the text and quickly after your review the book, go back and revisit the material. I promise you that with perspective, things change, even in the most minute way. Lets continue on.

The grouping of feminine is such that I don't want to leave out any one particular type of woman or individual. I do, however, recognize this may happen. Please throw your politically correct ideologies out the window for a moment. If you are a scholar or specialist—throw your perceived and learned perspective into a box for just a few and lock them away. Over analyzing will not help you to grasp what I am sharing here, it may paralyze you from learning actual. So take a freeing breath and read on.

Take a moment and absorb these groupings.

WOMAN

Female, feminine, nurturing, loving, supportive, competent, strong, well rounded in all things womanly, mature, full in spirit, curious, capable, insightful, intuitive, kind. She is a woman and she encompasses all that is strong and weak about herself, in every way both inwardly and outwardly. There are so many possibilities for a woman, the world is open to her at every direction and she only has to develop her world when she comes of age, utilizing her experiences and life lessons to be the whole and best person she can be.

TRADITIONAL [WOMAN]

Holds her particular traditional values, learned or perceived by her own sense of experience in her maternal world close at heart. She is the life and wife partner, could be mother figure that stays in the confines of boundaries of home, perhaps not literally, but in the way we structure our life. She leads the home, from a strengthened feminine perspective. She is empowered by her role. She is the orchestrator of systems that guide the family in maternal and feminine form. She may or may not work, but her priorities are in the home, could be cooking, cleaning, organizing familial projects and gatherings. She is a mother or maternal figure in the home grouping. Her views of the world are from the tense of Tradition, from the state of time which time doesn't shift view easily, a slower more focused and rooted space. She nurtures, strengthens, and leads under the direction of either her husband or her higher power. She is the driver and director of the souls that she touches and guides, bringing life to every day.

MODERN [WOMAN]

This strong, feminine woman is powerful, but could be weakened depending on perspective and other factors. She is in line with the times of now, and may be on trend with her views of the current state and function of the times. Her ability to maneuver the world comes easily, with a fluidity that seems timeless in its own right—in the moment, but it if not kept up struggles could ensue to attain the most Modern perspective on life approach. She as a Modern woman may navigate work, home, school, a husband or life partner, children or take some form of maternal role. Her approach to familial structure as it relates to the maternal aspect, usually leans to a more feminist, rather than feminine, perspective meaning that there is less emphasis put on the traditional role of the Woman's role in the relational structure, leaning toward but not all the way in the direction of the Feminist. She, as a Modern woman, balances her responsibilities in the home, with her chosen familial structure and relationships, while thriving in her role at work or in her working roles outside of the home. The Modern woman is comfortable and confident in her skin as a power figure as she defines it, without outer discriminating factors. She has the emphasized ability to steer from feminist influence; she is more independent in view in her role. Her drive is strong to independently nurture, guide, and impart within her familial role. Modernist perspective of this woman is more from the standpoint of being aware of the world around her, and those more advanced states of the world than it is being apart of the actions and progressiveness of the world state.

Because of her modernist perspective she is able to better navigate her strong femininity without crossing over to the feminist view of the modern state, and she is able to hold to heart a more traditional world perspective because she sees t the world in it's modern state.

FEMINIST [WOMAN]

She is removed from her feminine. She is the antithesis of the male persona, but in a woman's body and viewing things from the masculine female role. Her view is that she can do anything a man can do, but better, to the extent that she over emphasizes such ability to the extreme, bloating sense of self, often taking reality of every day world interactions to the point of unnecessary projecting self centered wisdom of that world view outward. In her womanhood, the Feminist is dominant in approach, masculine in role of business, home, and social interactions. Even in the case of maternal roles, the Feminist has strong masculine driving influence. In her strength, and fight for the retention of her feminist build, the Feminist woman is weakened in actual role for equality, as her driving persona is seen not as virtues to be drawn on and leaned on, but as a threat and completion for power. She is a self-seeking, self-serving, a self-surrounded personality of the world.

CONSERVATIVE [WOMAN]

She is reserved, outspoken yet polite in nature, direct but in rounded communication. Her focus is principled toward her virtuous nature, a nature that encompasses many facets of her life. She is protective but balanced in her approach; her family and maternal value systems are strong, grounded in her belief systems. There is no wavering of fundamental values both familial and social, her word and duty to self and higher power, or God is first and foremost. She is strong in her commitment to work, family, maternal and social connections, putting the relationship between them as a connectivity that will help foster balance. The conservative woman views commitments to family and relationships as fulfillment and completion of self, and as such she supports marriage, partnership, and unity in relationships. She sees value systems, the way in which she leads her life, both familial and maternal as a method of expression of truth, wholesome in nature. She is patient, kind, giving, tender in her approach toward others, but stands her ground, not in selfish and self seeking fashion, but in then need to fulfill her commitment to herself, her God or her higher power.

LIBERAL [WOMAN]

There is a way about a Liberal woman that has an energy of its own. She is outward, though she can be reserved and inward in her social structures, generally she is gruff and has abrasiveness about her dealings in social circles. Her approach toward work, business, social, familial and maternal aspects of her world are broad and she likely won't be shy to express her disagreement with others with little compromise on her views or terms. There is little in openness of views of mind or flexibility in feeling. When approached by a mirrored self or persona, she is all too quick to pick and look for lingering or faltering value systems that are not liberal leaning enough. There appears to be a sense or need to adhere to liberal value systems even if they are not serving the collative good as they self-purportedly say to do. The liberal woman tends to lend herself to broad social groups that encompass her own world view, in both familial and social elements. Maternal instincts and feminine attributes can be found in some liberal women, there lends to be less so of a pronounced form the more leaning toward Feminist a Liberal woman is. She is strong minded in her own view and right, she can hold varying social and economic views, though generally depending on which direction her views go, they remain somewhat rigid in standing. There is little in getting her to compromise where her Liberal views are rooted. Generally, her Liberal views root to either familial background or early experience, later on in life growing to see a more broad world there is in many times a shift in belief systems. Rarely is it the other way around. She can be of many facets, much like the conservative woman, only her value systems seem to feed self in the name of others, her desires come to fulfill self rather than the other way around. Many of her leanings socially might approve or express support of same sex relationships, no need for marriage, marriage of same sex partners, sex before marriage or outside of marriage, multiple partners, open relationships, and other liberal leaning lifestyle choices, positions, and views. This does not necessarily mean that she lives in that space personally; rather she may just view these social perspectives as being not only an option, but also a worthy cause to fight for should they be challenged, much like the Feminist.

In many cases the Liberal woman may have a faith base or even be spiritual or ascribe to a religion. One of the more interesting perspectives or traits of a Liberal woman is that she may not align with the more Traditional aspects and views of her own chosen religion, spiritual or faith in entirety, throwing out unneeded or conflicting philosophies, In many cases we might see the Liberal woman even justify actions or lifestyle against her faith. This sort of dealing with life issues is often times repeated in other areas.

The Liberal woman is not without contribution to our world, she holds her own, only it is weighted in a direction that should be viewed with caution.

AMERICAN[11] [WOMAN]

She is a citizen of America; she is woman, female, and feminine. Her drive is for herself, her higher power or God; she is for her partner or husband, and her family. Her allegiance is to the Republic. She is committed for the things that benefit her, her family, and her country. She cares about the world around her and her commitments, the nations of the world, though she preserves most the value of sustaining those things that preserve the future for her own, first and foremost knowing that doing so will benefit others. This is where her comfort is, in the safety and security of all the things fulfilling her duties as an American Woman.

After looking with an open mind and reading about each expanded "definition," if you will, my hope is that you see some driven lines between the different aspects of each respective focus. Now, I am sure this provoked some bias or perhaps stirred different thoughts and feelings within you. I am not asking you to say my definitions or views are absolute, rather I am asking that you hold these definitions within your mind as you move through the text. I think that when you are through reading you may understand the purpose. Think back on my definitions and your own preconception or judgments as you read through them. You can either write your own thoughts down or highlight where we differ, but the most important thing is that as we move forward you let your views go and go with the flow of what I am trying to share with you.

The Modern Conservative Woman, or in the case of Americans, the Modern Conservative American Woman we can throw in the definition of each section that pertains to the definition and call it a day. After analyzing the differences between Traditional and Conservative, I almost think that there really is not too much need to complicate things here. Traditional and Conservative overlap in ways that as you relate them to a person they really are almost so similar you might not be able to tell the difference.

As we approach a person who might be Ultra Conservative, you may be able to get away with calling her a Traditional Conservative Woman, taking the Modern out. The thought here is that she is so set back in the ways of Tradition and how things operate in the order of things of old that there is nothing Modernistic viewing about her. She may actually see and view any Modern Woman as being almost Progressive. I know we didn't get into that definition, but it is similar to that of the Liberal, and thus this is why I say she may not be Modern at all in her ways. This is all right really. Individuals are who they are. We, however, are better off if we can identify different traits, understanding the information and logic about these personalities, the lifestyles of particular women, and will be better equipped to interact appropriately with them.

Back to the Modern Conservative American Woman, she is strong, fearless, she sees the world as it is, and she lives within it but doesn't necessarily conform to the world. She is able to maneuver within the context of her surroundings at work, at home, or wherever she is with ease. She can see as well as identify different perspectives of those around her, even relate to them. Her drive to secure her person, her faith in higher power or God, and ties to maternal and feminine perspective are highlighted. She is expansive in her approach to family, devotion, and commitment to every aspect of her life. She sees value in tradition; in ways that are not too outreaching, they are proven and secure. The consistency of the world around her is lifted up and made strong by recognizing that value and also applying current real world scenarios to help her maneuver through her world. It is easy for the Modern Conservative American Woman to find both passion and joy in her life because her driving forces also feed her in her life, figuratively speaking. Those around her not only benefit but also thrive as a result of her positive attributes.

Love of country, love of family, love of herself and higher power or God, these all are those driving forces I was talking about. This is not to say that other groups or individuals do not experience these sorts of things or don't also fit within this description. I am merely trying to paint a picture for you as we move through the text.

This definition is actually Revolutionary. It will open up your mind to view facets of so many things within people you may have never noticed before today. There are traits, among which we fail to tap into when we communicate with others. We may also walk by someone on the street or be people watching, not realizing we can take in so much information, not just about our world, but the people in it, too.

There will be recognition that comes and you can outwardly see a person might be of a certain perspective deep within, leading you to be more patient. There might also come a rigidness about someone that you may see now. You may not see them as merely a gruff person here on out, rather you might see clearly their view from a time past, from an extended learning pattern that created this Liberal or Feminist perspective. This will now allow you to tailor your approach to be more available in a way to communicate more clearly.

You will see it. Let it resonate; let it grow your mind and in how you view these traits. It can't hurt, this sort of observing can really only grow you and your life view, if you let it.

Chapter Four

JEANETTE PICKERING RANKIN

O H, THE TIMES AND DIFFICULTY being a woman of any color. Times where women didn't have the right to vote, and in many cases, couldn't do the work they wanted to do to fulfill their dreams. The year is 1880. The state is Montana, Missoula County to be exact. Being born era where most women were Conservative at their core, this is when God brought us dear Jeanette Pickering Rankin. Now, not everyone will agree with me that Rankin, as we will call her, was a conservative. If we roll back in time, using my definitions, she very well could be a Modern Conservative American Woman. Her contributions by many may be viewed as progressive or liberal leaning. I, in fact, see what she did and how she approached her life, the interactions within her family, community, within the nation, as a more of a Modern approach rather than Liberal in nature.

As a child, Rankin, growing up in rural Montana had to help in the home, on the farm, all the while getting her education. Her large family and academics provided the foundation for a successful and blooming life through her formative years as a young woman. Rankin fished her high school years and moved on to get her Bachelor of Science from the University of Montana. The year was 1902, when she graduated. Given the times and career ambitions verses the availability of a young woman who was still single, Rankin took on other more appropriate rolls and jobs that were available to her.

You have to remember it is the early 1900's and being highly educated and a woman, it was not something that was necessarily the norm. Rankin was highly sought after and proposed to on several occasions. Being driven as she was, as committed as she was to the development of her mind, determined to put her skills to good use Rankin accepted a social worker position in San Francisco.

Her heart was for the people, her life, as she knew it was going to be giving to others. She saw it as a calling and a practical and solid fit. Harnessing this, Rankin went on to educate herself at multiple universities. It was at the University of Washington that Rankin became involved in the Woman's Suffrage movement.

In her activism Rankin saw a need, a need for women. She had vision. She had duty not only to other women, not just to her state, but also to the nation as a whole. In her work as a leader of Modern Conservative Women, her work in November of 1910 led to Washington becoming the fifth state to amend their Constitution, permanently enfranchising women. Rankin went on to organize the New York Woman's Suffrage Party. This conservatarian was blossoming. The following year, in a bold move, one many women dare not do, Rankin went before the Montana Legislature. She was the first woman to ever speak on the floor of the Legislature. Really quite impressive, I gather from everything I have read on the Suffrage movement that there were many uphill battles for all women pushing for equal rights to men and the ability to vote. Rankin would be no exception.

It would be several years before Rankin would see her first speech take root and grow, bearing fruit. The fruit was good though. In November of 1914, Montana passed historic reform, an amendment granting most women unrestricted voting rights[12]. Later equality would be attained for all women. August 26 1920, upon the passage of the 19th Amendment African American women were extended their equal rights. It took many more years and hurdles for Native American women of Montana and other states to gain their voting rights mainly due to issues relating to citizenship and their residing on land considered to be sovereign nation. There is another entire story that could be told about equality and actual rights, perceived rights, as well as the exercising of rights. This is not the story we are telling today. Today we are examining Modern Conservative American Women, their role within society and how with proper communication one can accomplish great things.

Rankin knew there was a time and place for every battle. For true equality this took time. The suffrage movement you see was not a liberal movement as many would like you to believe. It was not a conservative movement either. It was a women's movement. At the core it was a human movement, driven by women and enacted by men. As I see it, Rankin's effort was in support of human equality. Women were in the forefront of the battle for equality. While many may disagree I stand firm in that we as woman have a role to play like Rankin had in her early years. We as women need to ensure that our families are secure, that our identities in all areas of our lives are exerted and affirmed through our actions. We accomplish this through communication and our interaction with others.

With this direction of her life, Rankin surely saw many successes. Her impact nationally was vast. Mainly, Rankin made it evident that her work was specifically directed toward the advancement of our nation. Her desire to have women participate in the processes of government as a necessary one, that many of the shortcomings of government and policy were due to the lack of feminine perspective and participation. She affirmed that in her speech at a disarmament conference during the interwar period, "The peace problem is a woman's problem."

It was outwardly evident in her role during her tenure in congress that women needed to not only play a role in politics: it was their duty to do so. It was necessary in her view and by her actions that women were going to be at the center of strengthening our nation. There was a need in American society, and in the interest of World Peace women needed to get involved. This Rankin woman was something.

I had heard many wartime stories about her, mostly vague and as a youth. And as a younger person I always thought her as a democrat, a liberal. It wasn't until I started reading up and learning about the suffrage movement that Rankin was indeed what I define now as a Modern Conservative American Woman. Rankin was a powerhouse of a Republican Woman, in those times and at that stage in her life. She carried herself with dignity and she stood firm in her beliefs for Peace for America, for the longing that we as Women, we could play a roll in impacting our Republic.

In her life, Rankin was an exemplary approach to politics from the Feminine perspective for a good portion of her life, from a true Woman's perspective. She led and paved the way, but in a manner which some saw as Modern, but was not so brash that it prevented her from making an impact. She would go on many times through her role in Congress to further her position being a woman and being against war being a solution.

As time went and then the Japanese hit Pearl Harbor, Rankin saw one of the largest struggles of her career. The call to war was imminent. Rankin was the only member to vote against war. "As a woman I can't go to war," she said, "and I refuse to send anyone else." This rocked congress and there were shutters across the nation. Hers was a hard and difficult plight. She stood, when men caved, for what she believed was right. Hers was a dedicated life to serving as a Woman in public office.

As we see Rankin move through her life, the times become more volatile and woman, woman's rights specifically, transition through many different eras if you will. In her early life, through the prime of her working career and mid-life, we see Rankin as what I define as a Modern Conservative American Woman.

Now, the times of the world, wars and other painful times in world history occurred. A woman's role in society changed drastically as a result. We see, as evident in her actions, Rankin shifts her activism toward a more Liberal leaning around the times following the bombing of Hiroshima and before the Vietnam War.

It is unclear if perhaps the more conservative times themselves, given the era, in her earlier life, if this kept Rankin more reserved and conservative. It could have also been the constraints of the budding involvement of women. We certainly saw her bravery and courage, as well as Resolve practiced in her early and midlife. She approached the woman's role in activism with dignity and demanded respect with her feminine presence and demeanor.

As times changed, developing into the 1960s, she became more emboldened, and not necessarily in some views in a good way, perhaps it was also due to the massive amounts of activism of the times. The nation did evolve and move to a place where outward clash and a darker approach to human intellectual interaction was intensified. In part, her metamorphosis, the transition of the times, the drastic change could also have been magnified and even nurtured by the entrance of Media into the home. No longer was the slower pace of newsprint and evening radio the standard. Television, advertising, as well as the infiltration of propaganda on massive scale was most certainly growing roots throughout America, both in and out of the home.

So Rankin, as her later years approached began to be backed by large Activist groups influenced by herself and others who saw similar goals of furthering woman's rights, worker rights, among other human-interest goals of the emboldened Activist realm. Resolve, which Rankin once ascribed to in principle and in her approach to the calling for women, it started to dissipate and what took over was a more aggressive, less tolerant form of Activism, one which saw a shift. No longer was the goal to shape and influence government to empower women, the feminine to nurture and grow our political system in a positive way. It was now the drive to impact society as a whole and to push an agenda on the Conservative and moral fabric of American Society. There were outreaches and women's activist groups Rankin was tied to which most certainly can be seen in the underlying sentiments of the female Liberal and Feminist of today's age.

In her own way, Rankin is the prime example of how a truly genuine and good natured Modern Conservative American Woman can be pulled from a direction of productivity and good will with balanced and appropriate impact to Liberal and Feminist ideologies that appear to have been a negative draw on our great American Nation.

There is a certain level of understanding that must come by looking at her life. Whether you agree with what she accomplished through the different phases of her life, one must allot her an amount of respect. She remained consistent through her career. Rankin remained opposed to War her lifetime over.

There is also a struggle, for me at least, to reconcile why a person so influential in the circles of a Woman's impact and necessary role in politics would associate herself with groups that were essentially a war of the mind right here in the United States. Right on United States soil. Why Rankin would affiliate with any war, be it war of the mind or a war causing bloody wounds, the casualties are much of the same, really. The long-standing effects of riots, and deep seeded hostilities created in the 1960s through and on to the early 1980s have festered in the minds of Americans to this day.

As we have seen in the last decade, namely marked in or around 2008 and the incoming of President Barak Hussein Obama, this sort of hostility by different groups which she contributed to in part, indirectly. Groups from "women's" rights to the rights of other viewed "minorities" or "underrepresented" segments of society have been the unknowing or at very least unintentional recipients of the Liberal side of Rankin's work. The element of growth, gentle and slow evolving nature of her formative years as an activist, have less of an impact I believe. There is some part of me that wonders if she might ever take back any of the things she accomplished in her later years if she were privy to some of the acts of Liberal and Feminists of today. The Liberals and Feminists marching with grotesque signs, foul vulva hats, and so on.

Knowing at her core the drive for individual rights, especially those of women, I could see her viewing anyone's actions their own and they should be responsible for them. I could be wrong however.

If you have not read much on the true and real Modern Conservative American Women of yesteryear, please do so from responsible sources. There is much to be learned from their bravery, and balanced yet firm approach to activism. The suffrage movement had its conservative base and it had a dark side, but mostly it was a call for absolute equality. Which I see as being accomplished some time ago, at least here in the United States of America. It is up to the individual Woman to embrace her power and act on her equality and live, unashamed and unstopped by the minds and actions of others.

In her personal life, there are many speculations that Rankin was a lesbian. In my view, as she relates to our work, here and in this case, this is irrelevant. The idea that her work came first and her job and drive as a Woman, and as a Modern Conservative American Woman for much of her early life and remaining dedicated in her purpose, this has an admirable consistency to it. One lesson many women could learn from in some sense, in today's world especially. We as Women, and MCAW specifically, could take lessons in the sort of dedication to principle that Rankin lived out in her lifetime. The dedication to her family unit, community and government, especially during her formative years consumed so much of her time that there remained little time for a personal life of measure. Rankin lived a long life, passing away in 1972 at the age of 92.

Chapter Five

GINGER ROGERS

THE SIGHT OF A BEAUTY. The brains of a powerhouse. The grace of distinctively feminine features, reaching from the inside of a Woman's being to the outside world. All the light in a smile to fill the hearts in American homes during times when mothers and fathers were worried their children might not or would probably not return from war. She had a gentleness, a presence about her. Ginger Rogers was her name. An all-American Girl. An icon. She was viewed by some as a side-kick. I disagree wholeheartedly!

Hollywood didn't do her justice on the screen; she was a natural presence of all things great in the great ole U.S. of A. For my childhood, I grew up watching only black and white movies and old movies that came in color. One of my favorite actresses was this dreamy light-footed darling, Ginger Rogers. I looked up to her for years. I still admire her lifetime of dedication to her art.

I always wondered how this sparkling princess of a peach could glide across the floor dancing as she did. Her ability to navigate the dance floor and be a light among those dreamy male actors; how could she practice enough? Where did she find the time? She didn't. What you saw on the silver screen was most literally the feminine light from within this glowing creature of feminine perfection.

For those younger readers who only recognize the name Ginger Rogers, please go educate yourselves and use Google to look up her movies and read about her life. Ginger had the good fortune of being one of the greats of an era long past. She also danced and acted along side of some of the most talented men in recent history. Recall Ginger Rogers and Fred Astaire. Hopefully the younger folks recognize those two names together.

Anyway, let's get to it. She fires me up with inspiration just recalling her energy on the silver screen. The way she would turn her body about, the gesturing of her arms, the delicate and gentle nature she would use while maneuvering her hands.

Have you ever sat and watched people? Have you paid close attention to the position of their hands and feet as they walk by? As we move through the text and as time passes, bring to the front of your mind the way in which people interact. Pay attention to their facial expressions, tone of voice, their shoulders and arm gestures, their legs and the position of their feet. Just observe. Recognize the context of the situations they were in or where they were and what time of day. Hold it in your mind for when we look closer at human interaction.

There is a magical way Ginger Rogers would move. She was electric and full of presence. Her hands told a story about her life.

Without fail, you could see the power in her delicate fingers. Her touch and way, which she would interact with her hands alone, spoke to her kindness, on the inside. Ginger as we will call her, she had presence on the screen for sure, but beyond that, behind the story of her on film life you could tell the complexities in those hands of hers. Her personal life, the way, which she lived, her life in her mind and being it came out on screen with her hands, and arms.

Because I love dance, I know and have spent years trying to figure out where my hands need to go and how it is evident that it takes time to perfect the art of dance and the hands. After over a decade of dance in different disciplines, I can see the authenticity of her hands in motion. It came from within with Ginger.

When Ginger would act in the capacity of a speaking part and role you could still see the mannerisms and movements of her fingers, the gentle and feminine energy was there. An attentive as well as openness was present. Ginger would "connect" with people, both on and off the silver screen. The manner of which she would speak to other characters, leaning in, touching objects, adjusting her clothes, hands to her hair, whatever you might see her do with her hands, she displayed for the world to see the generosity within her nature.

Now, I had never met Ginger. I know a few people who have. They all only ever had high and genuine words of praise to her character as a Modern Conservative American Woman. Never once did I or have I heard of a Liberal or Feminist perspective as it relates to her. Yes, even in Hollywood it is possible to be a Conservative. Of course, we are talking years back, I know. Truly though, even in its hay day Hollywood was considered a place of debauchery and filth by many. Hollywood also was taken by

Communists and used in political propaganda campaigns. This is not far reaching at all. It is well documented in History.

There were struggles for even the more Modern of the Modern Conservative American Women of those days back then, even and especially in Hollywood. So, for our darling Ginger, her plight to hold standards in her acting, her career—going against the Hollywood Liberal grain was a tough one.

Ginger, born Virginia in 1911, came from an early broken childhood. After she was born her parents divorced. Her father took her out of the home unbeknownst to her mother. He kidnapped her not once, but twice! Shortly after, her mother got custody of Ginger. Ginger was raised in part by her grandparents early on, but later when her mother had remarried, Ginger was around her mother's screenwriting and the theater world in Texas.

Ginger went on to compete in dance only to end up recommended that she get into film. Oh shux, right!? After a few on-screen bits she was taken to by the American public. Our dear and sweet Ginger wouldn't be in film bits for long! She was swooped up and put to larger roles and ended up at Astaire's side, dancing into his arms. Oh shux, times two!! She was all sparkle by his side. Let's be honest, Astaire never looked better than he did with Ginger by his side. Never.

Like many stars of that era Ginger got stuck in a role rut. But that didn't stop her at all. She went on to win an Academy Award for best Actress in Kitty Foyle (1940) and a career in acting and dance that spanned fifty years, comprised of seventy-three films! Outstanding run if you ask me.

Getting to our focus, her Modern Conservative American Woman role within society. Ginger was dedicated. Now, given her multiple marriages many might say she was less than Conservative. I, however, can say with confidence that this is proof of her belief in marriage, traditional value systems and striving for love and the draw to finding commitment. All of this, in a world, a place, many now call Hollyweird! She wouldn't be the first to struggle to make a relationship work in hostile and Liberal Hollywood.

Among one of the things that strikes me most admirable about this Woman was her contribution to country. Her contribution to WWII was great. No, not entertaining the troops! No, her role, part of the role she played, was very personal in fact. Ginger had a large farm she had bought for her and her mother in Oregon.

We will expand on her contributions in a moment. For those who may be younger readers and are unaware of wartime efforts nationally in the United States I want to touch on something here. During the war, WWII, many people made sacrifices here in our homeland for our over seas effort.

Aside from giving up wearing nylons and stockings or being excessive in comforts of home, giving up certain medals and so on, many played their part in any way they could. Some volunteered their skills, others, even women, left the home to work and contribute in factories that spanned the nation. It was a unified time here in the States.

For Ginger, one way she gave back and helped in the war effort was the use of her expansive farm. She had cows that were a part of a dairy. The dairy produced a good amount of milk. So much milk the dairy provided the much needed milk for operations in Camp White. After all, soldiers need to be in tip-top shape!

The milk from the cows was her effort, part of it. I know it sounds odd. But it was! This makes you think, I hope. Ginger was human, not just a song and dance number. She was an American Woman. She loved to fish on her land, in the river that ran through it. She was of the earth, provided for her dear mother, she looked after country, and she was making the nation smile and laugh on screen. These are priceless gifts and contributions ones, which lived on, even to this day.

Ginger's political leanings led to much criticism. Many thought her mother was the greatest influence, but I see her as not being the dumb blonde, song and dance number that others don't seem to be able to let go of. In fact, despite one fellow employee saying, "I doubt that she could have told you the difference between the Republican and Democratic parties." Absurd.

Ginger took a stance on several occasions. In one instance, during the McCarthy hearings, it was said that Ginger loathed making "Tender Comrade," the 1944 film about four war housewives living together. There was a line within the film that she insisted be given to another actress. The line was leaning and praising communism and considered by many as propaganda-lite.

I look at the line as Blood Red, straight propaganda. It was so blatantly pro-communism I remember it from when I watched her film way back. So, the words "Share and share alike, that's democracy" would ring in history. The Director, Joseph Losey, was actually blacklisted. Yes, those were the times. I recall this from one show or another I had watched once upon a time, it was remarkable. The Director went on to criticize Ginger as well as her work. I told you, uphill battle. Battle of the minds, within her work there were people trying to use her art to further the Communist Agenda. And with Ginger, you know these sorts or situation poured into social circles off the job. Navigating such situations came with ease but at a price, too.

This darling woman was giving. She was so much more than we saw on the corny but entertaining music and dance routines on the silver screen. She had an authentic and organic substance to her. Ginger was relatable, natural, and magnetic. Strong, feminine, giving, loving, family oriented, she desired the best for her countrymen and nation, AND her mom. She is another of our Modern Conservative American Women. Ginger, our darling ginger, passed away near my town, in Rancho Mirage, California in 1995. God rest and bless her sweet soul.

Chapter Six

ZORA NEALE HURSTON

ORN IN NOTASULGA, Alabama in 1891, our next Modern
Conservative American Woman is Zora Neale Hurston. She
was a turn of the century revolutionary much like Rankin, only
completely different. Zora as we will call her, she was a voice for
many. Her natural ability to put thoughts into words, and words
to paper was one to be reckoned with. She had many dreams and
lived fully and completely in her work—but unfortunately, she
died alone and poor. Her gifts were writing, among the flow to her
paper were novels, short stories, folklore, all the way into the world
and work of anthropology to which her work was deeply rooted.

Her education was halted in her teens but she took to study
and entered Howard University, went on to Bernard College
and then on to Columbia University for her graduate studies,
something equality mongers might not see as too impressive of

a woman. Unless, of course, the year is 1928, you are a woman, still rather young, under 35 years of age and of African American descent.

Now, I am one to say, and many to this day do not like me for just this, but keep your mind open remember. Keeping your mind open for work to come later in the book is imperative. But I need to let you know for perspective of the book; I am completely against Diversity measures. I am also against Affirmative Action. My reasoning is that Equality is Equality.

Now, in the case of Nora, she is a historical figure and is special. I would like to use historical reference and context to highlight her plight. Her ability to overcome was second to none.

Really, women, working women of the early 1900's had a tough uphill battle, especially if they wanted to marry. Remember, that early on in American History and even into the early to mid-1900's women could work in many areas of society but only if they were single.

If women were single, there were areas within American society that would not allow them to work if the job was not seen as fitting for a woman. Certain fields were off limits. Should a woman be of the working type and she was to marry, she would give up her job to dedicate her life and time to the family unit. That is how it was, and in many Traditional American and Conservative American homes this is still the case.

So, in Nora's case, she was married to her work. Her work was her life and there was no letting go. She wrote her life away as many saw it. Indeed, her life is one to really spend time learning about, especially through her writing, which is beautiful.

She was highly criticized for some of her work given she was of African American descent. African American men, or as she referred to them, Negros, were enraged by her work. This is still the case. You see Nora, being into the study of Folklore and the human condition saw her roots as a positive and praised her roots. Nora celebrated her historic presence within America.

This is something that some of the more violent "Revolutionaries" of the 1960s and on saw as completely uncharacteristic of a true African American Woman. Nora, she has a powerful Modern Conservative American Woman's voice. She was proud of her father, her family, her roots. There was not a person on the planet that could deter her from her purpose.

In her life's work, in her dealings with others, Nora was not the norm, especially among her "peers." Quite frankly, she was an activist and one that was not pushy or making the way in the sense that others were within her community. She was subtle but honest; she looked at her roots as honorable and worthy, full of dignity and lives with future and promise. Unlike her peers who used the victim mentality approach and negative draw that we discussed when exploring the later part of Rankin's life work.

I applaud our lovely and talented Nora, her fearless approach to her studies, and devotion to her father, community, to her work. She is truly a dignified and talented Modern Conservative American Woman. Indeed, many in our "Modern" times could learn from the fruit of Nora's life. They could learn from the dedication, from the embracing of familial ties and peaceful expression of Equality for all that we now have. I am confident if Nora were to be living today she would have much to say of our human state of affairs and interactions. She would be both disappointed and proud. Our beloved Nora. One of the greats, for sure.

Chapter Seven

MARGARET THATCHER

A ND FOR OUR LAST LEADING LADY, one of the most notable of
our time, Margaret Hilda Thatcher. She is in a league of her
own, really. Maggie, as we will call her, was a Modern Conservative
Woman, for sure. I leave out American because Maggie was the
loveliest of women, powerful and dynamic, but not American.

Born in Grantham, United kingdom, in 1925, this hot rod of
a Lady graced us with her presence on planet earth. Not only was
Maggie a champion for Conservatism, she was a lovely leading lady
in her personal life. Again, many might argue some points, but
really, even the soviets couldn't argue with her uncompromising
stance personally and politically. Because of this she was dubbed,
literally, The Iron Lady, the Iron Chancellor, mainly due to her
Britain Awake speech, but it stuck.

This leading warrior for conservatism has more titles behind
her name than I have letters in my entire name. For the younger or

less politically astute crowd I will highlight Maggie's background just a touch. Aside from the obvious, she was a delicious orator. The way she would enter a room, everyone would turn to look. She had presence. She was a woman of substance. I truly believe she could speak with anyone about anything and connect on a human level. At her core, she was a real person, relatable, no matter her status in government. She had a genuine care for the people, one that reached into her very being.

She was a Chemist, then a Barrister, an elected Member of Parliament, and Secretary of State for Education and Science; she became the Leader of the Opposition and the first woman in the United Kingdom to lead a political party and became Prime Minister in 1979. Her accomplishments go forever, as it seems. There are months and months you could spend reading about her life in Public Service. Maggie was a true champion in her field and devoted to the people she served, on both sides of the isle.

Further than her political positions and service, this incredible dynamo found the time to be a mother and a wife. A daughter of a grocery store owner, Maggie knew hard work. She was a mother of notable accomplishment, raising two children, and twins no doubt. She had her children the year she qualified as Barrister.

Maggie's daughter, Carol had this to say in an interview:

"All my childhood memories of my mother were just someone who was superwoman before the phrase had been invented. She was always flat out, she never relaxed, household chores were done at breakneck speed in order to get back to the parliamentary correspondence or get on with making up a speech."

Superwoman. I can imagine Maggie as just that! If you watch her in video archives, she is amazing. I would see her on television as a child and stand in wonderment. Her grace was to be matched if one could—but they couldn't. The manner in which she would walk was always consistent. Her shoulders were confident and proud. Her chin was always straight, and her facial expression was notably open for an approachable conversation. She had the ability to navigate a room; her hands and arms were notably by her side or expressively up and open in a welcoming way. She was a master at communication.

There is even a historic speech where she speaks with fervor in her voice, her countenance is firm and unwavering, her eyebrows notably pinched together at one point—you knew she meant every word she was saying and there would be no moving of her oration and position on the matters at hand. A woman of pure substance, that Maggie!

Chapter Eight

TOOL BOX

A S WE LOOK AT WOMEN in history, specifically the women I described earlier. The displays of their lives, the sorts of backgrounds that become them, none of them ascribe to a certain region, really. More so, I think it is evident that these Modern Conservative American Women hold their lives in certain form. Their lives are lived according to a measure of values and tradition of sorts. We can see that all these women could compare in some way with women we actually know within our communities. I wouldn't be farfetched to say that we could examine ourselves and see a part of us within them and their lives. We may share some commonalities.

We really only went into each figure briefly. I wanted to share only truly relevant information to the book. It is important to me that I not waste your time in going over the material and use the text wisely. So in that, if you feel led, please read more on these prominent figures within our modern and recent day history.

What we will go into now really is just also scratching the surface of what I see can help you in your journey to discover new and better ways to grow in your communication, our communication really. There is so much out there that can be of use.

Over the last decade, I have been observing people and contexts of relationships as they relate to politics, the family and work settings, and general interaction between different groups of people. What I have noticed as of the last few years is that there is an uptick in tension amongst families. Women are not in the background—they are in leading positions, and often in uncomfortable situations within the family unit, trying to navigate interactions and communication. This is an area of struggle as of late. I know it is a long-standing issue, but our nation is transitioning again as it did in the 1960's and the 1980's.

As we face these shifts, as a people, and as a nation we must adapt. It is important to recognize that needs of people change and with that we have to recognize those needs and approach people differently and accordingly. I am not a psychiatrist or a anthropologist, I am not formally educated at university in these areas, however, in my profession I was well mentored. I took every communication course available to me. Literally, I spent years mastering the art of human interaction. It is an art, in my opinion. Because I am not licensed or skilled to counsel on issues I will be sharing my experiences with you and what I observed. I will share with you how I came out of certain situations or how I see things or situations.

There are ways we can learn about things from experiences and I really want to impart to you what I have learned so you can benefit. In the "TOOL BOX" I hope you will find valuable tools that aid you in your everyday communication, not just as a person, but as a Woman, and as a Conservative American Woman. Whether you see yourself as a Modern or Traditional Conservative American Woman, I want you to take away from this immediate and applicable skills and fill that "TOOL BOX" up so your family, your work and home life and your situation becomes a more fluid and productive space.

We will be looking at and going over some skill sets that I learned about in my trainings of old and used for years and unknowingly had refined to make my interactions easier from day to day. From there we will delve into the really exciting and sort of silly terms that I came up with to help you remember and easily practice the tools you are learning.

First off though, I want to bring to the front of your mind again that you really need to think about the thoughts going through your mind. Let your preconceptions go. Release your judgments, release them for now. The nagging in you that says this is too hard, leave it be and make this a fun exercise of new experience. Remember, most new things bring challenge, but they also bring excitement and new revelations.

I am not sure about you, but in my life and around me I have experienced and seen families arguing unnecessarily about issues that are important, but don't have to cause tension in the family. It has been too often where I have seen friends bicker over the latest news and not be able to move past it.

Literally, in the social media world of today there have been families broken, friends lost and fights that were unrecovered from as a result of a political or social issue that came up. These sorts of issues and conflict may not be able to be avoided entirely. But, I truly believe in my heart of hearts that in America today, there are Women, Modern Conservative American Women who can lead us from this path of destruction. I truly believe that if you want to make an impact in your home, in your life and community or workplace, you can. You can heal relationships by just being you, within your own circles, in various way and contexts all you need are the "TOOLS" to get started.

The "TOOL BOX" can be visualized if you like. It can be put to a picture if that is easiest for you to relate to. Simply the "TOOL BOX" its self is your mind. I will say that again. The "TOOL BOX" is your MIND.

OK. Think about that.

In your life, you have come to different situations and circumstances, you have been faced with challenges that seem too big to face. Possibly, we faced situations that are uncomfortable or make us uneasy. There might have been instances where we face the unknown and situations are just not sitting right with us. There are many cases where words could be used or expressions used that hurt our feelings where they ordinarily wouldn't, there are uncountable variables that could be present. Communication, interaction, reaction, response, how we process things in our lives with situations and experiences, it is simple. It comes down to one thing, Your MIND.

Your MIND is your "TOOL BOX."

Wrap your mind around this for a second. Imagine you are going to work. You have to perform a certain job that required tools. You would bring the right tools, wouldn't you? Now, what if you knew that you were going to a job and you might run into extra issues that could require special tools to get things done should something go awry. You would show up to the job prepared, right? It would be important to think and prepare accordingly. You wouldn't want to have to leave the job and risk losing it because you were unprepared, right?

This is exactly it. This is life. Be prepared. Make sure you have the right tools in your "TOOL BOX" to get the job done! Look, we all understand there are things, situations that are out of our control. Even the best trained psychiatrist struggles with emotion and life here and there. Life coaches may have their life in need of coaching. We all suffer from the human condition. What I am saying is, if you can prepare, do prepare. What is there to lose?

Let's get back to the good stuff. In the case of the "TOOL BOX" there is such a thing as the wrong tools, too! For now, let's focus on what we need, how we can grow and the positives that are needed to adjust our way of thinking about what kind of tools are already in our "TOOL BOX."

Ok, readjustment time. Refocus your mind on right now. Take a deep breath. Take another deep breath. Alright, let's think about the "TOOL BOX." Your MIND. What is in there that you use to communicate? What equipment do you currently have? What equipment is outdated or broken that we can refresh or replace? What equipment do you need that you don't have? These are really important questions to examine because these are the areas in our MIND and life that may need addressing.

I will list for you some "TOOLS" that we use to communicate:

» our bodies

» our thoughts

» our emotions

Yes, it is that simple. Life does not have to be complicated.

Ok, let's refocus again. I want you to take a deep breath. Take another deep breath. Now, think about the "TOOL BOX" and what is in it. Your body is used to communicate so many things to other people about what is going on in your mind and how you are feeling. Likewise, their body is giving you loads of information on what is going on in their mind and emotions as well.

This is simple stuff. Do not over complicate it. If you want to get into the science, you can, there are shelves of books on this, but again, this is why I am sharing with you what I have learned. Let's keep it basic.

Your mind, your emotions, drive your bodily responses. Without going into technical things because that is not what we are really doing here, let's think about this. If we can control our bodily response by monitoring our thoughts and emotions could we better communicate with people and see improvement in our relationships? Absolutely.

BUT it is equally important to understand you can only control your own thoughts, emotions, and bodily responses. Re-read that. In reality, what I have experienced and learned is that our responsibility with action and reaction ends in what we do and say. Re-read that. In reality, we have very little ability to impact someone else and their response, they need to take responsibility for their own lives, actions, reactions, and emotion.

There are ways, however, to try to maximize the little margin we do have to impact someone's response to our own actions and response and that comes with expanding on the "TOOL BOX."

Ok, it is time to readjust. One more deep breath.

Let's go with what we know. You have the base equipment you need in your "TOOL BOX." You have body, mind, and emotions. Those are the basics. The foundation and core. Now, let's expand. When you face a situation or experience that is problematic where does your mind go, how do you feel, and in what way does your body respond? This is important.

Example 1: If I am faced with toast that burns in the toaster and I am running really late for an appointment, this is what the situation may look like:

- » Mind: Oh man, I am not going to have time to eat now. How could this have happened?

- » Emotions: Confused and Frustrated

- » Body: Eyebrows furrow/pierce, eyes narrow, mouth clenched, my ears may move if I clench my teeth, shoulders drop, and my arms irritated reach to clean up the mess. My breathing may increase.

Example 2: If I am faced with toast that burns in the toaster and I have no place to go and am relaxing for the day, this is what the situation may look like:

- » Mind: Oh man, bummer. I'll make new toast.

- » Emotions: Mild irritation, resolve and move on.

- » Body: Forehead rises, mouth may shift, a mild sigh, shoulders may drop, my breathing won't change much.

What is the difference between the two? They both have burnt toast. One aspect is time, as it seems. Really, there is nothing different. The perception is different. Pressure of time might be the issue, but is it really? Think about how you would respond in both situations. What you would think, feel, and how you would react. This is vital.

In different areas of your life I want you to think about these things, at least become more aware of them. For us to be well rounded we must be aware of our world, and how we operate within it.

In order for you to repair, replace, and add to your "TOOL BOX" you need to be able to identify what is in need of repair, replacement, and added to it, right? Right. So be aware of your everyday thoughts, emotions, and reactions. Journal if it helps you. Even being aware of how you think, feel and react will help your interactions with others, believe it or not. Awareness is key.

Alright. Now, take a deep breath. Ok, take another deep breath. Let's go ahead and reverse the situation here. It is morning time. You walk into the kitchen and your mother is making toast. Instead of you going through the following thoughts, emotions, and bodily reactions your mother is experiencing them. Now, read them below:

Example 1: Mom is faced with toast that burns in the toaster and she is running really late for an appointment, this is what the situation may look like:

» Mind: Oh man, I am not going to have time to eat now. How could this have happened?

» Emotions: Confused and Frustrated

» Body: Eyebrows furrow/pierce, eyes narrow, mouth clenched, my ears may move if I clench my teeth, shoulders drop, and my arms irritated reach to clean up the mess. My breathing may increase.

What is going on with you when you enter the room and see this:

» Mind:

» Emotion:

» Body:

Example 2: Mom is faced with toast that burns in the toaster and she has no place to go and is relaxing for the day, this is what the situation may look like:

» Mind: Oh man, bummer. I'll make new toast.

» Emotions: Mild irritation, resolve and move on.

» Body: Forehead rises, mouth may shift, a mild sigh, shoulders may drop, my breathing won't change much.

What is going on with you when you enter the room and see this:

» Mind:

» Emotion:

» Body:

My best guess is that if you look at each of these both realistically, and if you are human, your response will be night and day to help your mom. I could be wrong and there really is no right answer here, only that you can start to recognize the differences, comparing and contrasting situations to help you begin to bring awareness to your life situations.

I would like to suggest you further look at your different reactions by replacing the word mom with other substitutions. You can use dad, friend, sister, brother, daughter, son, friend, grandmother, even colleague. In each case your thoughts and emotions as well as reaction could change slightly or drastically, depending.

What am I getting at here, you might be thinking. Well, what we have been discussing is Modern Conservative American Women (MCAW) in history, their lives and communication. We are currently in times, which are requiring us to be more aware of what is going on around us.

As MCAW, we are faced with many situations in our lives, not just at home, but at church or at our place of work or volunteering. It could be situations we face while we are out and running errands or interaction with our children or our spouse or friends.

The way I view this is, we as MCAW are the feminine and necessary role players in society that lead in our homes in a way that men don't (in general). We have a natural responsibility and obligation to nurture the world around us, specifically and most importantly in our homes first, to impact and grow it in a responsible way.

We are it, MCAW, we are on the front lines in the fight and revolution to take back our family units, repairing our broken family ties, encouraging our children and supporting our partner or spouses, strengthening our communities. This all starts with you. This starts with your "TOOL BOX," your MIND. In order to do that there must be awareness; there must be change, repair and growth.

We can change the above scenario one thousand times using different people over and over again. I can outline so many different things right there, but I think we should move on. Save that segment above, bookmark it, or highlight it. Go ahead and revisit using different variables over time to help you identify your own thoughts, emotions, and reactions from both perspectives.

Over time you will see patterns. Note them for future reference if you like.

Alright, let's take a deep breath. We have looked at the basics in our "TOOL BOX" and we now know how we can start to understand what we think, how we feel, and how our body responds not just when we encounter situations, but when we see others encounter situations as well. We can now better identify how we might think, feel, or react to others in different situations.

You see, if we replace the scenario with a political interaction or a familial political interaction, or something as benign as someone cutting in front of us in line somewhere, the basics don't change on how we analyze the situation. So, take your time in figuring out how you and your "TOOLS" work.

After you have done all your observation and recognition, you will be able to progress to a point where you can start to make adjustments to your thoughts, emotions, and actions that more accurately respond to a situation.

Trust me, there have been countless times where I was faced with a situation where I could have overreacted or responded in an inappropriate way. Instead, I took a slow breath, and started adjusting my thoughts, bringing down my emotion and this in turn changed my body's reaction or what experts might refer to as body language or in the case of the face, micro expression.

What did this do for me? Well it depends on the situation, and we will go into that later when we explore the actual terms and different ways people react. It can do many things, I have even seen it neutralize otherwise intense interactions.

There is a great deal to be said about your ability to recognize your own strengths and weaknesses. Your goal should be to be balanced, building your weaknesses up and relying on your strengths to carry you through the process.

I believe we all have space for growth, no matter what life space we are in. If a person thinks they don't need growth or have things to learn and build on, well, DING! DING! DING! There is the weakness right there. But again, you can only change you and recognize traits in others to improve YOU. In improving yourself you will in turn improve the world around you by default.

Chapter Nine

BOTH SIDES OF A COIN

TWO THINGS I TRY to remember about life. One, the obvious almost always has hints to it that remind you of number two. Two, most of the time in life the answers and solutions are simple. When in doubt start over, going back to number one.

This sounds funny, I know. You probably have heard similar things before. This is because you have. And if you haven't I want to know what rock you have been hiding under. No, I am just kidding. Truth be told though it is true. The more complex we do try to make things at times the harder life and the process of life we are in becomes.

Through the book, you hear me say things like let's keep it simple, let's take a deep breath, and some other things I say over and over again. It is to remind you, program your train of thought. It is to bring you back to a space that is slower, to a space that is in the present. This is in an effort to work on controlling your own mind and becoming aware of what you are doing and thinking. There is a reason behind it, I promise.

Ok, let's get to the nitty gritty. There are two sides to a coin. Yup, most of the time the sides are different. They are however both part of a coin, right? They serve common purpose and they have the same destination, right? Right.

Well, think of Democrats and Republicans. Right now, and in recent history we have seen a greater disparity in how each group thinks or what they believe. Specifically, the last 8 years since 2008, we have seen an alarmingly quick divide in moral basis for the two groups.

These aren't the only political parties in the United States, we know that, but what we have witnessed is that these two groups and people that fit within these two groups are completely polarized in many instances. This is not a healthy trend, not for you, not for other families or communities, states, or the nation.

Only a few times in United States history have we approached positions where heated interactions hit a boiling point and went nationally. Luckily, in most recent history we have not gotten to the point of civil war. It is unfortunate, however, that we have seen civil unrest to the extent that we have within our communities. I am hoping with this book and the involvement and activity of Patriots and God fearing MCAW that we will begin to see better communication and see healing in our families and within our nation. With that in the forefront of your mind, lets revisit the Democrat party for a minute.

The Democrat Party lends itself to be comprised of mainly Liberal Women and Feminist females. I leave out the word

Woman when I refer to Feminists, because by definition I am not sure that the term fits in partnership with the definition of Feminist, because a true Woman is feminine. I am sure this might upset some centrist Democrat Women who are not Feminists, but I assure you I am not referring to them. I hope I am not losing you. Recall the definition of Woman if you are confused.

The Democrat Party in general, Liberal and Feminists alike, have belief systems which I strongly believe are breaking down the American Family Unit. Many beliefs that I believe are eroding the moral fabric of our American society. No one has to agree, but that is how I see it. In general, many of their stances are in direct contrast to the Republican Party and the Traditional and Conservatives.

Some of the issues that divide this coin are abortion, same sex marriage, LGBTQ rights, socialized medicine, borders and national sovereignty, gender equality, environmental policy, global warming, gun rights and the list goes on. Now there are always exceptions, and people have to look at this level headedly. Some Democrats may be Pro-Life, just as some Republicans might be for Same Sex Marriage, or SSM. This is in itself another issue we have to deal with. Generalizing is a lose-lose situation.

I am not saying we need to go PC or soft speak on the issues in order to have conversations and move through and build relationships with different people, what I am saying is we should approach our understanding of those we meet with open eyes. We should approach each person with availability of understanding.

The divide that keeps us apart is breaking our nation apart. Something has to give. What does that look like? As we see that our values and beliefs differ as MCAW from Feminists and

Liberals we can identify where someone stands on an issue or perspective and understand where they are coming from.

Mind you, this is in a situation where the person is approachable or it is safe to do such a thing and discovering the differences from conversation. I, in no way, am suggesting you confront people about their stances on issues, this could provoke someone, causing unnecessary divide even further. My ideas and learning have shown me there are better, more constructive ways to interact.

In most cases, as a MCAW you will be about your day and come in contact with someone who might be reading a magazine and make a comment. You may be at work and a co-worker might mention the latest political hot topic in jest. It could also be that at church a hot topic subject of moral stance is brought up and it is in conflict with your beliefs. There could be a host of situations. Learning to recognize the situations are just part of what needs to be done to combat and shift the situation for the betterment of all involved.

Remember, what we are seeing is a divide on the issues. You will probably identify that divide when you feel your gut urge you on something. That "gut feeling" if you have ever heard of it is real and accurate. Pay attention for a few weeks to the issue, to the situations and you will become more in tune with it.

Back to the two-sided coin. One thing we should also acknowledge as MCAW is that our devotion is to being in touch with our current state as a nation. We should be inline with our conservative principles and values, which encourage betterment of self, family, community, and country of course.

We are American as well and because we are, we hold certain values to heart. If you forgot, review the definitions earlier in the book. We should also keep close to our hearts that we are women, and as women we play a special and divine role within the family unit. A feminine role that only women can fulfill. Our commitment and duty is to all these things and more.

Your own beliefs may be slightly different. I understand, but my point is this: if we hold true to these things, we must encourage good things for our families and communities, the states, and the Republic at large. This includes communicating and keeping the interests of both sides of the coin in the forefront of our minds.

Even when the other side of the coin isn't on point with the same values, so long as we have done what we can to communicate, to promote proper discourse, and encourage appropriate dialog, we have done our part as MCAW. There is little room for silence as a MCAW except where words only add divide. More often than not silence is a tool that should be used when listening. We will talk about this later on in the book.

The two-sided coin if you recall is one where the other side is in belief of very different views from your own and those of your family. Just because they have certain views does not make them right in their thinking. Likewise, they may view your positions the same way, you are wrong and they are right. They may stand just as firm as you do in their beliefs. They, in general and due to many of their belief systems, could be more aggressive or direct in their approach with your on their beliefs. Do not be alarmed by this. There are ways to create healthier dialog, and there are also times when you should just accept that people will think and act how they choose like we were learning earlier in the book. In some cases, you have to learn how to recognize situations where it is not only better to back off and walk away or let go of a topic, moving on becomes increasingly important. It is ok.

For the conservative cause, it is better to stand firm in your beliefs, holding strong to your value systems and walk away knowing you didn't compromise yourself or the cause with losing your temper or cool, bringing shame to your family by saying something out of character, or acting in a way that is contrary to your beliefs. Your life is a direct testimony to your stance as a MCAW. The evidence is in every step you take. No one is perfect, we all make mistakes but let's make best efforts to learn, taking the highest ground possible.

Here is a story for you. One day I was at the grocery in line. I had what I call my "All-American" Hat on. My hat is a Trump hat from the last election. It is adorned with pins given to me from friends and fans from all over the nation. I have a Ted Cruz pin on the hat that a fan made for me, specifically with red, white, and blue rhinestones. It is super cute. There are several law enforcement, Department of Homeland Security, Immigration Customs and Enforcement pins, there is a Hillery For Prison pin, Republican Women pins, you name it, I have it on my All-American hat.

Now, I am standing in line with this hat on, it is post primary election but the general elections have not happened yet. So, the heat is on. I am about 5 foot 2 inches short, and in my workout clothes. Super casually dressed as many might view it. There I am, little ole me, with my hat. Do I look scary? Am I a threat to anyone? This man behind me, he says, "Oh my god, do you see her hat?" Really? Does he know I can hear him? It was so hard to not just start laughing and say something snarky back. But what would that say about me? About what I stand for? What would that say about the people I would vote for? How does that speak to my character?

Instead of mouthing off or saying something rude or just saying silent, I made a choice. I turned to him and asked him, with a bright and shining face, "Oh goodness, do you like my hat? Isn't it great! I love wearing it, it is a great conversation piece." I swear he turned as red as the stripe on the American flag! His chest went up, he looked down at me, lifting his nose and his arms moved inward. His brow did furrow. Now, after all his body response, his lips tightened and he turned to look again at his friend, his face red, not only was he embarrassed he was not sure how to respond. What could he say? Want to know what he said? He nervously laughed, getting uptight and turned and said I guess so.

Do you know, ladies (and gents), right there was another opportunity! Without judgment, and he could tell and so could everyone else, I asked him a question. I asked him, "Do you know who you are voting for yet? I really would like to hear your views." One word: Dumbfounded.

Yup, Mr. I am gonna intimidate this woman didn't know what to say.

He did respond, actually, he mentioned he wasn't sure and he had thought about voting for Bernie.

AND AGAIN, ladies, no need to be hasty, this creating conversation and promoting conservatism is not just about you.

This poor, dear little big man. I said to him, wow that is interesting, he isn't my guy obviously but a lot of people your age tend to favor him over Hillary.

Then it was my turn in line.

Our entire conversation lasted much less than a minute in total, the impact of our conversation will last a lifetime, I guarantee it.

This is exactly how it works, ladies (and gents). In good will, with the opportunity to have a good and possibly fruitful conversation with someone, with many people looking on in interest, I opened the door for dialog, actual dialog, when he just wanted to intimidate me. You don't have to be sassy or rude, there is no need to insult or trash anyone, or give a snazzy come back. There is a need to have conversations, to not back down because of intimidation.

All too often I think, on our side of the coin, MCAW it seems are encouraged that remaining silent is the better option. Yes, there are those times, but mostly you can be quietly and genuinely direct about your beliefs and stance while maintaining dignity and respect of those around you. IMPACT, think Impact.

Swaying public opinion and the opinion of those around you is easier if they don't have reason to doubt what you are saying. If you keep the power in your hands by asking questions, by trying to understand their points of view. All of these things play to your character as well. Being of sound choices, admitting when you are wrong at times, ascribing to learn more about an issue. These all play into your role as a MCAW.

Keeping an open mind does not mean you have to change your mind or shift your belief systems, or that you are flipping to the other side of the coin. It only means that you will hear another's perspective, understand where they might be coming from. This only helps you understand them so you can make clear decisions in how you interact as well.

Again, don't fear gaining knowledge about someone or their beliefs. They might just be impressed that you care enough to hear them out. Trust me, you will know in your gut if someone is just wasting your time or jerking you around by telling you about themselves or what their beliefs are. More often than not they are glad to have someone listen and hear them out. They may also be in need of information or be on the fence about an issue they are talking about.

When dealing with the two-sided coin, because someone can literally be the center of the coin; I prefer to be cautious in some situations. For instance, I have some libertarian beliefs, given that I see myself as a Constitutional Conservative this can cause some issues surrounding Freedom based beliefs. Many people out there are in this same situation. There is a hefty percentage of people who are Libertarians or other parties who may not hold your same views. They may also lean Liberal in some areas and Conservative in others.

It is no wonder why, with the polar divide we currently have in the nation politically, that these "others" or "centers" of the coin get caught in the balance.

Brass tax: what I want to make sure of is that you as a MCAW or as a CAW or even as a TAW, where ever you are in how you view yourself within conservatism, that you can recognize and identify different leanings, varied approaches to the issues and carry yourself in a way that will help not only the conservative cause but boost your confidence and ability to communicate with your circles and space.

It is important in your roles that you flourish, that your familial circle runs smoothly, that you are able to face conflict or disagreement, equipped and able to move forward, being an example to either your children or others around who might be impacted by interactions and your communication.

Chapter Ten

OUT WITH THE OLD

THE DAYS HAVE PASSED when we could stand by idly and let the world shape its self. As we saw with Rankin, there were opportunities where she bettered the Republic for Women, Conservative Women can look up to that stance. In the case of her later years, she approached them with far too much of a Liberal stance. The times had progressed, sure, but really there was no need to push equality after equality was attained legally. To continue forth with Women's Rights issues caused, in my opinion, a great deal of future break down.

Equality is equality. It is as simple as that. Out with the old thinking of pushing Woman's rights outside the home. We have equality at the ballot box. We also have equal job opportunities for education, employment, for pay. I can hear brains flipping out as I write. This is why the chapter is called "Out with the Old!"

Take a deep breath. Let go of your preconceptions. Let go of your old way of thinking for a moment even to think for yourself. You can read all the statistics by the experts and evaluations by number crunchers on both sides of the funding blocks of different organizations, each one massaging the message to fit their funding perspective. Really think about your life, comparing it to even one hundred years ago. Think for yourself on this for a moment.

To say that we have anything less than equality as women, it is just flat out irresponsible. Notice I say we as women, we have equal OPPORTUNITY. The reason I say this is because we do. Equal opportunity does not mean equal outcome. Life and opportunities demand effort behind them, which help to attain goals. Life is exactly what you do with it. Life is what you put into it. Period.

Our lives as Women are filled with the opportunity that many, many before us never had. We have it, we only have to embrace what has been paid for with the lives and effort of many before us. This reaches to ever area of our life, really. Make a note of what you are thinking right now.

As we take the time to learn more about of ourselves, letting go of past perceptions only good things will come. Even as we learn new skills and grow our minds, facing new challenges we will see good and positive change. Out with the old, let it go.

The struggles are real. Yes, they are. We as women face so much in our lives, especially given the standards we adhere to in our lives and our commitment to conservatism. The world inches toward more immoral and unethical positions every day, this may impact our space, but we can face it and we have the ability to combat it. We should look at though where the struggles are specifically so we can let go of what we learned and grow further.

What I see as MCAW is that, now, we are pushing to preserve and even restore our rights within our homes. Freedom to choose your own medical insurance options, and coverage's, Freedom to raise your children as you see fit, in a school of your choice. In the work place there may be challenges faced, within the Church even there have been moral breaches that many people are struggling with, not just in this nation, but around the world. Don't lose hope. Fight and resist the thinking that it is all too much. Push back against the ideas that there is nothing you can do to change things nowadays. Those are not productive lines of thought. Let them go.

We are going to take a few moments here. I know it seems funny, even strange but follow me for a few minutes here. Many years ago, I learned a technique and I have been utilizing this now in other areas of my life where I didn't realize that it could benefit. Now this isn't hocus-pocus. Really, it isn't some sort of new age thing. It is actually one way that we can help our brain to process information YES! Our brains are complicated.

I can't begin to explain how this works scientifically. I will leave that to the psychoanalysts and those who study the brain. What I do want to point out though is in all my reading, learning, being mentored, it was told to me over and over that our brains cannot tell the difference between an actual event and when we think about that same event after the fact.

So, I will explain this a little bit more for you. When a person experiences something, anything, good or bad, the mind sees it, the person feels it, and the body is impacted. After the fact, when that person gets in the car or wherever they go, if they think about what just happened, it is near and equally as exhilarating or upsetting. Sometimes it can even be more enhanced than the initial experience because the person had time to process the experience. There is a reason why this is. The mind cannot distinguish the difference between actual experience and the imprint and memory of the experience. If you do not trust my insight here, do your homework.

This is why I urge you to LET GO OF THE OLD and unnecessary thoughts that are holding you back in your life, in progressing of your mind to good and helpful things that benefit you. Let go of the old train of thought, let go of the old preconceptions that have gotten you to the point where you are now. Now, you are seeking solutions, my hope is you at least try to enact some changes. If you want solutions, really want them, try new ways of thinking and looking at life. If you continue to do the same thing, you must take responsibility in receiving the same results. It is that simple.

I want you to take a moment. Take a deep breath. Now, all those thoughts when you are talking to your girl friends, guy friends, husband, children, or perhaps colleagues, when you get into insurmountable conversations and interactions that seem too big to overcome—do this for me. Picture each of these thoughts in your mind. You can do this one at a time or collectively. Now, using your mind and thoughts, take your figurative hand like you are grabbing into a huge bag of cotton balls, instead, picture those thoughts of defeat—picture each thought in your mind.

Now, figuratively, reach into your mind, and with a big handful, grab those thoughts with your hand and figuratively hold them tight, imagining these thoughts are in your hand. Imagine that you have each and every defeating thought in there. Now, take your hand, filled with these thoughts and throw them! Cast them away from you. Throw them far, far away. As far as you can, using your mind and visualization, imagine that those thoughts have left your mind and are flying through the air, far far away, and can barely see them. And then, you see them disappear. They are gone, forever. They are no longer a part of your life. Your mind is refreshed and relieved, completely rejuvenated. You now have room to grow.

You have chosen to grab the things that were complicating your mind and your life and make new ways for yourself. This is a new and special moment in your life. New perspective is coming. In trying something new, in stepping out you are actively acknowledging that you really want Revolution in your life. You want to make impact in every facet of your life. Give yourself credit right now.

Chapter Eleven

IN WITH THE NEW

WITH THIS NEW TURN in thinking, the openness to impact our family, improve our interactions within our home, our communities, our state and within our Republic, we are enacting what I call Revolution America! Seriously, what you have chosen to do in your mind and life is a Revolutionary act! It is that simple. Really, our ability to impact our country begins in our own minds, with the way we think and operate.

Think about this, your friends, or colleagues, your partner or husband, perhaps family members, how many of them do you know and think can make improvements in their life, in the way they think, interact, in the way they live? How many people do you know have such big issues that need addressing in how they think that it impacts others but they don't even see it? Or perhaps, not only do these people you are thinking about not see they have problems with how they think and how they interact with others, they wouldn't change a thing even if you talked to them about it. They might even get defensive. How many of these people you are thinking of actually know they have issues but refuse to change? Or perhaps they have tried to change but for whatever reason they just can't break through the patterns of thought, mind, and body and emotion reactions?

Recognize that you are part of Revolution America. Really if you think about it, you are Revolution America. I am Revolution America. Your conscience decision to reexamine your life, reevaluating the way you approach your own mind, your thoughts, emotions and bodily reactions or shall I say, actions. That decision is a Revolutionary act.

Revolution America starts with your mind. Revolution America moves outward with every change you make which impacts those around you, pursuing a more healthy and balanced approach to your life as Modern Conservative American Woman (MCAW).

Let's face it, every action we make as Women especially MCAW, they all have a roll out effect. Those around us are recipients of our influence. This is a dynamic and prolific focus right here. If you really and truly understand the way you and your actions radiate outward every day, all day, you will be more active in your decisions through the day. Even in the things as simple as we talked about earlier, like the toast. These simplistic things will be magnified allowing you to choose wisely how you will act verses react to situations.

Actions, bodily actions verses reactions or bodily reactions are an important area to highlight right now as we begin to transition into our more specific areas of focus. Our communication discoveries and reprogramming go hand in hand.

Please recall the burnt toast scenarios. In each situation, we encounter there are ways our thoughts impact our emotions and bodily reactions. Please draw them to mind. In our "In with The New" focus we should highlight the positives if we can here on out. Where we had recognized negative reactions and patterns, where we had seen a draw and response that was not productive and helpful we should correct our responses.

When I say correct our responses, I mean that when something happens, good or bad, our thoughts should be reconciled. As a Modern Conservative American Woman (MCAW), or a Traditional Conservative American Woman (TCAW), our thoughts should be in line with our core value systems.

For example, if you are a Christian and your thoughts are impure or of leaning in a direction that is not in line with scripture, acting or reacting in any way on that thought has no use to it. Well, it has value, just not the sort of value we want. We should practice grabbing the visualization and discarding the thought, moving our mind to a healthy and balanced thought which will lead to a more healthy and balanced emotion and bodily response. This is vital, no matter your background or religion. As a person, specifically a Modern Conservative American Woman (MCAW) or Traditional Conservative American Woman, we should hold ourselves to the highest standard. Recall that these practices all start with you. It is only when people see you living by example that your personal Revolution will spread in America in a positive and lasting way.

Back to action verses reaction. When you react to something, when you allow your thoughts to take control, leading your emotions with little effort, your body follows almost instantaneously. It is imperative that you harness your thoughts if you want to make long-term gains in your communication.

The reason why is because this near automatic chain reaction sends off cues to other people that may be in the room or around you. Their reactions can then end up in an avalanche of unrecoverable chain of events, or put you in a position where you have some clean up to do and your relationships will continue to struggle. So, work on this. Only when you master your thoughts will you be able express appropriately what YOU want to say or show in your action about the situation you are being faced with.

Remember when you were visualizing your response to someone else's situation and reactions, there was a bit of delay. Training yourself to be present and aware of each thought, and the emotion and bodily response will slowly allow for you to grow to the point where instead of being reactionary you will be taking action! When you have control of your thinking you can suddenly have control of your emotions and bodily actions (instead of reactions).

In tense situations, it is best to have control of your thoughts, emotions, and bodily actions. It is a skill that will take time. Don't get frustrated. Make the time and effort to learn about yourself, how you think, how you feel, and how your body responds. You will be the main beneficiary; your family and other areas will benefit as well. Obviously, you want long lasting personal change and to benefit yourself and family, as well as the Republic in your personal Revolution so keep at it.

Ok, take a moment here. Take a deep breath. As we move into bringing in a new and fresh way of looking at things, we should take a bit of time to look at some of the issues that are tough throughout the nation and through the world right now. Now, these modes of human interaction, observation, and communication are highly complex. There are literally books piled on books about some of the terms we will touch on next.

In this book, we will only scratch the surface. We will focus later on more relatable and easy ways to look at communication and then get into the core of how all of this relates to our familial and social interactions with tension and politics.

Within the modes of communication and human interaction and recognition there are many models that are followed. There are literally dozens and dozens of techniques that have professionally written articles about them, refereed journal articles, as well as scholarly research to back them up. Two of those models will be explored now. Recall, I have personally and professionally put these to the test over my career, and in this recent decade I have used them to communicate within certain social circles and political interactions. They are proven. But they are very difficult to remember.

I myself am not licensed or in any way going to tell you exactly how to use them, rather I will share with you what I have learned about them and how they worked for me and if you would like to research or learn more about them, I encourage you to do so.

Myself, personally, I found a better more practical way to apply similar techniques that are easier to remember and that I will share with you and how and when I had to use them.

SOLER AND SURETY

As we look at two terms, understand that they are used in many different settings to enhance and encourage good communication.

Two acronyms we will look at are SOLER[13] (Egan, 1975) and SURETY[14]. Both terms are long and actually extremely clinical. This is why I go into later what I came up with for everyday life, and in the workplace. Also, I give reference points above where you can go to different papers that discuss each term to learn their exact definitions as well as their use. Please, I encourage your learning about these different techniques after reading my book. The mind is one of your most valuable assets, and is effectively and practically what I call your "TOOL BOX," if you recall. Please fill it with useful tools.

Let's get to it shall we! Don't yawn. Learn. Take a deep breath and absorb. You are about ready to take a look at your "TOOL BOX" again! Trust me, when you are done with all of this you will have a new-found confidence, if you don't you will have to write me and share your experience, for sure. Here we go…Time to power down.

While SOLER has been around for over forty years and been proven, there is cause to believe there may be more effective ways to communicate in different settings. For instance, most times when there are intense or charged circumstances it is vital that there be certain levels of personal safety taken into consideration amongst other things.

Now, when there are sensitivities and charged emotions there may also be a need for a more sensitive approach, this is where I personally believe the need for SURETY came in to play. The human condition needed addressing, empathy and emotions as well as the need for connection is a very real and necessary thing within the mode of communication.

Not every setting is dry and without emotion. And specifically, what you and I are addressing today within this book is the need for Revolution America to happen within your mind and its ability to reach outward. We are dealing with family and friends as well as others who may be closer to us than say colleagues or a stranger on the street or someone we are treating in a professional capacity at work. It all comes down to context, as I see it. So, let's look at both terms separately first.

SOLER is a term that was developed back in the 1970's. In general, it is used within clinical and nursing settings. It is also used within many other institutions nationwide and globally. More often than not I have seen it used due to its long-standing record. It is consistent in that it is widely used and recognized. This is not the reason communication techniques should be relied on, in my opinion. Yes, it is effective. Yes, it is best used when it is fully understood and mastered, and practiced within every day interactions. Generally, this approach for me has performed at its peak within professional settings. Here is the breakdown of SOLER.

SOLER stands for the following:

S: Sit

O: Open position

L: Lean slightly toward the other

E: Eye contact

R: Relax

Right off, just by the mere and outright acronym, which any lay man can see topically right off that there might be issues with how this particular communication technique might be accomplished. Let alone, it is long and most folks might have a hard time remembering it. So, let's go through the letters.

S: SIT

In most situations you and I might find ourselves in we most likely will not be sitting. In many cases if you or I are sitting, it might not be in a formal setting where you could naturally and easily turn to the person you would like to communicate with. This poses a peculiar and possibly uncomfortable means to communicate, straight off. If you are found to be in a situation and want to utilize this technique, I myself have found that one can suggest the individuals sit down and talk about this. Or something else that can be done is rather than sit, substituting sit with Relax. The important part here, in my experience, is that the individual involved in an engaging situation and the conversation are better served if you show that you are relaxed, the equivalent of sitting properly for proper discourse and conversation. Exhale.

O: OPEN POSITION

In many cases, you and I may be on our way somewhere, we may be with family or children or like I mentioned earlier, I was insulted behind my back at the grocery store line, and loudly. What Open position means, most times, is when you are practicing the "S," your arms are not crossed, your shoulders are relaxed and your arms remain open, not crossing your body or person. Your hands could be placed on your lap loosely, they could be on the desk in front of you, but most importantly your arms are not closed. Closed refers to your arms crossed, shoulders down or down and in, and position where the message being sent is that I am not happy about communicating and I am not going to receive what you have to say.

In the case of being caught while in a line where I was, I turned around smiling and friendly. My arms were open and they were moving and held in a way that communicated a calm and relaxed state of communication, they were welcoming interaction. Had I closed and locked my arms, even saying what I did and how I said what I did, my arms could have ushered in a much different and possibly hostile response. It is an important acknowledgment here that we should make to Open verses Closed positioning of the arms and body with our body response and body language.

L: LEAN SLIGHTLY TOWARD THE OTHER

This is an interesting term that has been used, abused and botched as I have seen it professionally and in other forms of interactions. Look, you and I, in layman conversation and interactions at home or out and about, leaning in could be dangerous depending the setting and who we are talking with.

Within the context of work, depending on your profession and type of job it may be entirely beneficial in some cases and not appropriate in others. I think it important to stress here, even after years of studying this and putting it to use, I myself see the L for leaning toward the other as more an expression of interest than anything.

The suggestion in body language is that you are again, not "closed," you are open to discussion and interested in what the other person has to say. You are actively listening and engaging them in conversation and you care. These last few things may or may not be true. Let's just be honest about that, ok.

Each situation is unique. This is especially true as it relates to, say, your child verses your mother in-law who is upset by something personal or even a political disagreement you might have with her. It might also be true that if you are at a political rally or conference your situation may have its unique flavor, you may or may not care and leaning in might not be a good idea. In any one of those cases it is good to recognize the type of situation you are in, the thoughts going through your head, the emotions you are experiencing, and acting in a way that is situation appropriate.

For the L, I have at times, like in the case of the angry man in the checkout line that stood over one foot taller than I am. I have thought long and hard how to approach these sorts of situations. He was more than one foot taller than me. He felt the distinct and pronounced need to insult my hat and I while we were in a tight public place. That in its self is brazen.

So, when I described how I responded earlier turning, I didn't zip around with an attitude, I approached the conversation with ease. There was a smooth and gradual, natural turning while communicating that took place, right? Absolutely! The last thing I wanted was a situation where I got hurt or where a scene was caused that didn't benefit what I want to accomplish as an activist, which is proper discourse! So, my leaning was a natural turn toward him, with a natural and open stance while proceeding through the checkout line. It was effective. Each case is unique and should be handled with care until you master technique.

E: EYE CONTACT

Well, this is a doozy, especially given our topic of conversation in the book. Eye contact is necessary. Yes. What does that look like in a confrontation type situation verses a situation where you are caught off guard verses with your child, relative, or spouse. I firmly believe this too is contextual. There are ways you can look at a person with more or less sensitivity. There are ways you can make eye contact that are intimidating and confrontational.

There are also very natural ways to make eye contact that are welcoming. Now, I won't say that you need to smile at everyone because there are situations where this may not be appropriate. However, there may be cases where you can naturally maneuver the conversation while making relaxed eye contact that encourages connection, reaffirms you are actively listening and engaging in productive conversation. It may take time and practice to master the balance here. In many cases though there may be times when piercing eye contact might be entirely appropriate.

For example, if you need to be observant of an individual and they are staring you down, it might be good to get a good look at them, letting them know that you see them; of course, this too is situational. In my experience, some level of direct eye contact should be made no matter the context and situation. To give you an idea of what I mean, there have been times where I might slightly take my eyes to one direction or another or look at a person's face while using my peripheral vision to watch their face as well as their body language and other areas surrounding both of us. This is important to stress because some people are really sensitive to direct eye-to-eye contact. For instance, your mother might not feel comfortable talking to you if you do not let your eyes unlock, especially if the conversation is only mildly tense, it may be an intimidating stance for you to take that won't necessarily help the conversation's direction. I suggest you pay attention to how you interact with others and where you look over the course of the next few months. Observe and log how different people respond to your specific focusing of your eyes in each situation. It will give you some personal insight that can help in your body action section of learning. Eye contact takes a long time to master, not just in reading another person's eye contact patterns, but mastering your own ability to control your body, where you look and how you look as it relates to your eyes.

I want to touch on this for a moment, and it really does not relate too much to SOLER specifically, it mainly relates to the eyes in general. My belief is that the eyes are the window to the soul. The eyes hold a great deal of power in communication. There are many things you can tell about a person while looking into their eyes. Given this, it is important to approach the expression of the eyes, the communication they both receive and give with the respect they deserve. To use them for malice or intimidation, in my opinion, is irresponsible and shows a lack in morals and character.

So please, when you are learning about how you use your eyes and the expressions you make and how those expressions make people feel, use the expressions that naturally come to you. Do not on any level create situations to test out expressions or any such thing. It is most important for the sake of communication that you always, as a MCAW or TCAW approach those around you with dignity and respect and within the confines of absolute authenticity. Ok, let's move on to the next letter.

R: RELAX

Relax is used in many different texts for communicating techniques. It is over worked and over emphasized and seems to be the last focused on skill referenced in many disciplines. I know when I worked in Specialized Human Resources at the University and I was faced with certain situations, the very first thing I would do is a body check. And on my body checklist I would think to myself, literally, "exhale." Really this meant, RELAX, Erin, REALX! Most of the situations I encountered while in industry and academia, before I even became an activist, were very stressful in nature. People were generally in crisis mode. What do you do? You relax.

Yes, it is that simple. If you go into crisis mode you are of no use to the other person or yourself. So, in the case of children, or mothers or colleagues, angry protesters, a Liberal or Feminist trying to confront you, or a general deep confrontation, just Relax, focus, and be calm. Keep your mind available to what is going on in that moment.

I hope that makes sense, and we can go into this further as we touch on the other definitions of terms coming up.

As you can see, SOLER is a useful means by which to remember what steps can be taken to more effectively communicate with another person. Within SOLER is the resounding need to listen to the other person, to show that you are actively listening by your body action or body language. Learning about this further can only help you on our quest for Revolution America, so by all means do your homework on this term if you found it intriguing and useful.

SURETY is a relatively new term, one which is contrasted with SOLAR in many professions, especially nursing and the medical field. Some are saying SURETY should replace SOLAR, the forty-year-old "proven" communication technique. I say "proven" because I have heard that reference from colleagues over the years. I think of the term, "If it ain't broke, don't fix it!" But in the case of SOLAR, I think I was sharing with you where it has some flaws outside of a structured and professional setting. In a setting where you can say, "Let's sit down and talk about this for a moment," or you have a patient or person who is already sitting or lying in place, of course this would work, but in a laid back or around the town interaction, this particular skill set order and form needs revising. Also, in the case where people and situations need to be handled with empathy or listening requires that an element of emotion is expressed there is little to be shown for practical use here, in my opinion, at least in the Acronym's entirety as state and in order. So, let's get into and examine our next acronym, SURETY

SURETY stands for the following:

S: Sit at an angle

U: Uncross legs and arms

R: Relax

E: Eye contact

T: Touch

Y: Your intuition

S: SIT AT AN ANGLE

Yet again, we are faced with this "sit" thing. I get that not all situations are sitting. Did you get that? Sit-uations. Ok, I know, let's not waste time. But really, in a clinical setting, even if you are faced with a situation as a nurse or clinical worker, sitting may not be a practical option. If you go later to the original or follow up research and text, reading the full definition and terms it can certainly be seen where they are going with the reference and we understand this. I would still like to stress the clinical setting and professional offices are not always necessarily the context of which these terms are used in and applied.

Where I see this "S" is put to better use is in the quick style expansion of the acronym. Sit at angle is far less dry and already shows us that there may be further explanation of the acronym that lends it to being more relevant and useful in real world situations. It is correct, in that, sitting straight on can be intimidating and in many instances lack certain availability.

There also may be a derived sense of superiority if a person goes to sit across from you and sits straight facing you. Think about it for a moment. If someone sits across from you at an angle, it may appear as if they are relaxed, that they are perhaps somehow engaging you in away with their body action (or even response) that says, I am approachable.

There is a welcoming to sitting in this way, and non-threatening as well. In turn, if you are in a situation where you are talking with someone standing up, standing directly in front of them may be seen as confrontational, however, if you are slightly off center and relaxed, the openness for communication may be greatly enhanced.

U: UNCROSS LEGS AND ARMS

Surely this is a far better and less dry way to put this acronym! It is useful and self-explanatory. When you use the U in SURETY it stands for Uncross legs and arms! Voila! Really, how hard is it to understand this. It is similar almost the same as in SOLAR's

O for Open, only it has an openness to its description, doesn't it? In many ways this definition is the same only what it expands on is the lower extremities. This is highly important to recognize. Crossing any extremities, even slouching can give off many nonverbal cues to the person or audience you are communicating with. It is essential we expand on the lower extremities—the legs—to highlight what wasn't covered in the other terminology earlier.

When you cross your legs, there is a message being sent, like it or not. There is an unavailability that exists. Crossing the legs shows, usually furthering up other nonverbal body action or language that says, I am guarded, or superior, perhaps I really don't want to discuss this. Messages are being sent. I encourage you to observe yourself in situations and take not of how you react, also note how you respond with your body in certain ways when others change their body language. It should give you a good indication on what body action and language you can use better or different in specific situations. Again, this takes time to start recognizing, just like your thinking. None of this comes right off the bat. These changes will take active and consistent practice. I am sure you will start to find patterns in the way you respond and then when you change and open your body for communication, crossing your ankles verses your legs how people respond differently. There will also be a different response from others if you stand feet together verses about two to three inches apart as well as if you are standing in a more passive stance of four to five inches apart. Pay attention my lovely Modern Conservative American Women. This is so important!

R: RELAX

This is pretty much on board with the other acronym so we won't address it too much, only if you notice it is not the last in the list. It isn't because the creators realized how vital this was to have earlier in the lineup. I stand my ground in opinion that Relax should have been the first of each of these acronyms, but you know, I am not the scientist here. I am merely a user of the techniques, and now someone who is sharing her experiences with them.

E: EYE CONTACT

Now here we go again. Eye contact, one of the first things that should be done when interacting with others about any topic. Eye contact shows interest. Eye contact shows, or can show, active listening depending on expression. Eye contact shows empathy, if the situation needs it. Eye contact can express many things and contribute to your communication and conversation in more ways than you think. Please take the time to practice making eye contact, with purpose.

Remember, I believe Eyes are the window to the soul. When you make eye contact, what you are thinking is very important. What you are thinking and feeling often displays in the expression and intensity of your eyes. With this in mind, take note and practice making eye contact with people you interact with. Doing so will help you in your journey to mastering your body action and body language techniques, at least that is my experience personally.

T: TOUCH

Oh, now we are talking. This is a good one, especially for those of us MCAW or TCAW who are mothers, daughters, friends, or otherwise more social and feminine communicators. This could also lend to volunteering confrontations or conversations and all sorts of scenarios that we might run in to on the job even.

Really, Touch relates to a sensitive interaction where instead of leaning like the "R" in SOLER we might casually or gently touch an arm of a person or interact making actual contact to express empathy, active listening and communication. The definition is a bit more developed than that, obviously. On the whole, touch provides a mode of communication (when appropriate) that relatable as well as "real." When used organically, touch is a practical point of conversation, especially within the context of family or friends.

I would like to highlight like I did earlier that there are cases where it may not be appropriate to use touch. Remember the giant on isle 3 of the grocery store? You know, Mr. Insult? In that situation, even as casual as the conversation ended up going, as friendly as everyone ended up talking about my All-American hat, I wouldn't have used touch in our communication.

Very easily I could see someone reaching over, touching his arm while they maneuvered conversation. As for me, there are several reasons why I wouldn't use this technique and one of them is that I personally, as a widowed MCAW in many ways lean toward the TCAW in the area of touch. For me, personally, to touch a man I do not know joking around in public while making light and redirecting political conversation is inappropriate. Some may find that strange, but that is my choice. Really, personal space and safety are paramount, especially when dealing with strangers and outside of the home or office situations. It is important, especially dealing with Revolution America, our minds, the interactions and communication with others that we take our roles seriously as MCAW. We should always put our safety and the safety of our family as a priority.

Y: YOUR INTUITION

Perfect timing! Intuition. There might not be a better way to steer your personal Revolution America than your Intuition. Your intuition is always going to protect you and it will never steer you wrong. Read that again. Yes. That is correct. Please think about this for a moment.

I will in brief explain what your intuition is for those who do not know. When something is happening, there is a little voice, an urging. It is cautioning you or directing you, your intuition is the voice that steers you in a way that helps you. Your intuition is the voice that guides you to solutions and safety. Your gut as people might also call it. It is the very first voice that comes to you usually. And what people refer to when they say, "Trust your gut!" It will help direct your path on navigating situations and steering your communication, but you have to pay attention to it. Now there is another thing, and it is your conscious mind, it might tell you, "Wait!" it will caution you but only after your intuition or gut has urged you in a certain way. Generally, your conscious mind will undermine your intuition and confuse you. Not always, but it isn't always accurate. This is where the long and tested saying, "Don't second guess yourself" comes from! Now this lesion is not an exact science, but if you take the time to, again, study your thoughts, your emotions, and your body actions and body language you will start to see the evidence specific to you. So, bring and keep this to the forefront of your mind. It will come in handy.

So, in this way, the acronym SURELY is far superior in my opinion. The reason being that there are so many variables and subtleties in nonverbal communications, subtleties that only your brain might be able to process quick enough. Your intuition could more than likely kick in, showing you what you immediately need to know to respond to a situation in a split second of time. You can provide your mind with all the training it needs and awareness and skill sets it can use, but in the end, your intuition will be the quickest to pick up and read the situation. After that, as the thoughts roll through your mind and you discover they are balanced and decide to allow certain feelings to be expressed or not and then use your body actions and body language to communicate appropriately and you are all set up and ready to roll.

Most of what we see with these two acronyms SOLER and SURETY is really a processing of practiced skill sets, ones that you can test out and master. These both, after perfecting and if you like them, you can put in your "TOOL BOX" and use them as needed. They both have upshots to them that will prove useful in many area of your personal Revolution America, be it when you deal with your teenager and a LGBTQ situation they encounter at school and they don't know how to talk to you about it or if it is dealing with the school itself and its administration as it relates to similar issues. You will find that the acronyms change but communication techniques only vary slightly and mainly that is due to topic and the context of the situation.

Because some of these areas get heated, especially in the circles of Conservatives verses Liberals, or even Conservatives verses other Conservatives I had to find a quick way to remember some of the sets available to me in my "TOOL BOX."

What I did was find a way to package everything so it became easy to access under pressure. Serious, for me, at work it was easy to refer to my tools, it was a controlled environment. But at home, around town, at public events, when people didn't have to be so restrained and they could just go off, I had to find a better way to process information and be quicker about my responses. Gut and Intuition weren't enough on their own, even as quick as they are.

Also, I knew I had learned so much and because of the tensions in America over the last several years I wanted, rather, I needed to share my knowledge with others about how to better communicate. It is my duty. There is little more important than communication and preserving relationships with those in our family as well as within our communities.

I have to share with you a story. The new wave of acronyms hit me one night, out of the blue. I had already put them together and was using them daily, only I hadn't named them just yet. Kind of funny, right?! Like I said earlier, I like simple and easy to remember things. Period. I need every day things that will work in real life, in the real world. My hope is you do too. My desire is to help make your life easier, letting you skip some of the learning I had to do to get to this point.

We have a long up hill road here in America. There are so many conversations that need to be had. The right kind of conversations. There has to be a positive and productive way that I can share with you some more "TOOLS" for your "TOOL BOX" that can help you in your Revolution America. And then it happened...

Here is the dig on the night when they hit me. Those darn acronyms. Some people dream of puppies and I dream of politics and acronyms. So strange, but it is truth! I was a Saturday night and I was dead asleep. I must have been dreaming because literally, they woke me up! I sat up and said super loud, "I GOT IT!" I know this sounds bizarre, but this was seriously a Revolution America moment for me.

It was the space where I found terms where nearly every conservative woman has something in common. The true Revolution America focused MCAW, she is fed up with bloated, pork filled government and has a desire for reduced size and scope of government...

Right! Can you give me an "AMEN!"

And there they were: LARD and SKIM. Yes, you may laugh at it but you will remember them. Think big and fat (gov): LARD, and thin and skinny (less gov): SKIM, they will provide both large and narrowing results for your communication angles. And this is what I dreamt. So, I decided to put it to "pen."

Seriously, I know you are laughing right now. But I think about, read, and study current and historical politics and surrounding subjects nearly 24/7! Truly, if I could come up with better terms, I would... but this is it! It works, and if it ain't broke, don't fix it, right?! Right.

Getting to brass tax, we have to help one another. Restoration America has to happen and it starts in your mind, remember?! It then reaches to others using good and fruitful communication techniques.

I could go on and on. But I promised at the beginning of the book that I wouldn't waste your time. I warned you about training repetition though, so you can't say I didn't warn you about that!

Ok, take a moment. Take a deep breath. We are almost to our next learning session. While you may think that no one situation is created equal, that family situations and work context are not on the same level, all relationships are deserving of respect, especially from the Modern Conservative American Woman's perspective. Your personal growth from adding these "TOOLS" to your "TOOL BOX" will be instrumental to your success as a MCAW, no matter your role within our great Republic. And they are a synch to remember! Unlike the others we went over.

Political interactions in the home are tough. We are faced every day with situations now it seems where we have to converse about topics that didn't ever really have to be discussed before. This in itself causes issues, because there is not only one issue up for discussion or proper discourse, there seems to be several topics at a time introduced that are hot in today's social media. It is a circus out there and it has been for several years now here in America. We need solutions. Real ones that work!

When these topics do get brought up at home, or at work, possibly at a function or public gathering things can turn tense. I have seen it time and time again. Being able to utilize easy to remember acronyms like LARD and SKIM will help immensely, especially in politically heated confrontations and conversations. Remember that. LARD stands for "Listen," "Acknowledge," "Respond," and "Discover." SKIM stands for "Smile," "Kindness," "Intuition," and "Maturity."

Let's get to it!

Chapter Twelve

THINK BIG

WHAT DO WE AS MCAW despise just about the most? Big, fat, bloated government, that's what! And so, LARD was born. When we are dealing with people, certain people who are heck bent on forcing big government ideas, forcing issues that infringe on the freedoms of God fearing Americans across our nation against their will, we have to approach them in a way that will appropriately address the angle from which they are coming.

Look, there are literally millions upon millions of angles and ways and directions that a conversation could go based on variables that are ever changing, so I can't possibly address every single one but I can certainly group them so you can picture how this works. You must be equipped and impact your world. Your Revolution America must make impact.

Ok, take a deep breath. Now, I want you to work through this in your mind as we move through this. My goal is to equip you and your "TOOL BOX" with "TOOLS" that will help you in your interaction.

LARD stands for the following:

L: LISTEN

When someone, anyone approaches you, of course you need to relax. Of course, your Intuition uses your inner self and pre-programmed "TOOLS" from your "TOOL BOX" to kick in within milliseconds, yes. More than that, as all those things are happening, and your thought process starts, something must have happened that forced or encouraged engagement. Did someone talk to you, call your name, say something, bump into you, email you, whatever it might be, as all those other "TOOLS" are kicking in, one of the first things you want to do while observing, is listen. Saying what comes in to your mind, especially if confronted in a blunt or unexpected and possibly abrasive way, is not necessarily the correct answer. Your body actions and body language as you recall from earlier says so much on its own. At the core, it is imperative that you listen actively. What does that mean? Recall all the letters from our previous acronyms, active listening is eye contact, leaning in, open body action (including arms and legs), and possibly touch, depending on the situation. Nodding may be a part of active listening. It depends on the situation. Active Listening from the get go is about making that first part of contact a productive and meaningful one. Practice active Listening even in positive conversations. Note the reactions of those you practice it with. Was the conversation more or less productive. The more comfortable you are with keeping your legs uncrossed, and arms in an open position, the more often you practice Listening rather than jumping in to defend, explain, or simply have a say the better off you will be when difficult situations and conflict arise. Also, when you want to take action to speak with someone about something, you will have a notable confidence about you, which will encourage a more positive outcome, especially when the person goes to respond and you immediately start really listening, genuinely to what they have to say.

A: ACKNOWLEDGE

Wow, Revolutionary, is right?! Acknowledge the person confronting or engaging you. This doesn't mean to get in their face, this means when you are actively Listening to what the person has to say, you acknowledge that you are understanding what they are communicating to you. It happens far too often that wires get crossed and people completely misunderstand what is being talked about. If something is really important to another person, they will have no problem with you making sure that you understand what they are trying to say. Trust me, if they are going through the trouble of communicating, especially in an intense way, they will love to hear that you are understanding them and what their wants and needs are or where they are coming from on an issue. And then, return to active listening. Many times, after you acknowledge what someone is trying to communicate they will want to clarify or expand what they are saying. Let them, if it mattes to you and to them and is productive conversation, great! So long as the conversation is moving in the direction of understanding and possible solutions, this is a good thing. It is not always the case that conversations move toward resolution, but that is the goal.

R: RESPOND

Responding should be the natural progression of the conversation. At times, I have been in a tense conversation and I might just instead of saying, can I respond, I move to nodding and saying something like, "hmmm, I understand what you are saying, but I don't agree. We all share different points of view." You see, you have already gotten their seal of approval that you understood what they were communicating and why, now you are moving to share your view. Sometimes I have even "Let it go" like we did the thoughts earlier by saying to the person, "Well thank you for sharing but I have things I have to get done, it was nice meeting you." Of course, depending on circumstance and who it is and context that might dictate how you address the situation. Overall though, after you respond, if you are not sure how things are going in the conversation you can further it up with more active listening. There is something that the human condition lends to: people love to hear themselves talk, and they love an audience. There are studies, and we won't go into them, but they are out there. The studies show that in a conversation, the person who speaks the most is most often the person who thought the conversation went the best. Look that one up! It is fascinating. So, respond, then listen again.

D: DISCOVER

This again, is one that people do not see coming. After you respond you can ask more questions. Authentically and genuinely inquire why a person thinks the way they do. People want to know that you care and you take an interest. You do not have to in any way agree with what is being said, on the contrary it opens the dialog and shares that you care. At this point you can return to step one: listen.

Taking these steps, even in some uncomfortable situations and conversations can insert the human element, piercing hard hearts and showing that you as a MCAW see them as valuable. For many people that is really what they want. That is what they are longing for. They want to know their views or opinions matter.

Remember, practice makes perfect. There is no right and wrong here. There is only perfecting the long-lost art of communication and being Revolution America in your home, in your workplace and community, state and so on. The more healing that comes to relationships the better shape our Republic will be in. The more clearly we can communicate in the business world, the smoother things operate and efficiency increases. These are all winning in my book.

There is no loser from you being the best Modern Conservative American Woman you can be. Standing up for your rights by being able to better communicate and navigate relationships, this can only be another win. If you have children, your children and those around you learn by example. What better than to let them see be a success and also have them learn healthy communication skills. It can't hurt them, that is for sure, this is my opinion of course. Your personal Revolution America begins with you.

Chapter Thirteen

THINK THIN

S KIM STANDS FOR THE FOLLOWING:

S: SMILE

I love this. Smile. The face, specifically the mouth, is a powerful tool. There are certain nations where smiling is rude. America is not one of them. As a MCAW, I see it as part of your feminine persona to smile naturally, especially when approached by certain people. Now, I did LARD and SKIM because not all relationships are business and political in nature and not all are personal or filled with intense activist type interactions. Many forms of conflict or areas you need resolution in or may come in contact with as a MCAW will be at home, out and about, at volunteer centers, or possibly within a work space. Your smile, your mouth says so much about who you are. It is easier to approach someone if you know they are pleasant in nature, so when you come in contact with people, Smile! It will cause a great shift in your interactions with your children, family member, even in other relationships around you. Suddenly, and please take note of this, suddenly you will find that most people smile back. The conversation lightens, too.

Be genuine with your smile, giving the gift and energy from within. People can tell if you are fake, make an effort to find the pleasant space for a smile when you talk to people—it helps. One more thing, when you talk on the phone, people generally respond better to you when you are smiling. Try it. One of the thoughts behind it is that the pitch or tone of your voice changes when you smile. In turn your conversation shifts and changes, causing a lift on the direction of the phone call. Try multiple times and see if you experience a change with this technique. Be sure to make a note of it.

K: KINDNESS

It is not enough to just smile. When I talked earlier about being genuine and authentic, I meant it. Your inner emotions come out in ways that people can see, not just notably in their observation of you and your body actions and body language, it is also exuded in ways that their brain picks up in the form of micro-body expressions, so subtle they may not even consciously recognize they are seeing your body actions, especially when it comes to the face and facial expressions. Authenticity is so important.

No one wants to work with or have productive communication with someone who doesn't care and is grumpy all the time.

What we want to promote is growth and good will. We want to see communication thrive. One way to help communication thrive is through Kindness. Kindness and the willingness to help other, or share, thinking of how they might feel, all these things show in the way you think, which is evident in the way you feel, which ultimately ends up manifesting in how your body action or body language is portrayed or shown outwardly.

On the whole, if you are kind, it shows. When you are kind that means if someone is struggling and you are looking to communicate with them on an issue you are understanding, you listen, you are empathetic and that may show by touching or sharing.

Kindness does not mean you have to be a pushover, you can be gracious and welcoming, even kind while still maintaining healthy boundaries in conversation. Especially if conversations get tense, kindness can extend to promoting further in depth conversation, building a future in a relationship that will better the situations ability to have follow up interaction and communication.

Even in the case of Mr. Insult from isle 3 in the grocery store, I displayed kindness. I rocked minds that day by not reacting in the way he and others expected. Furthering up his rudeness with an extension of an olive branch of sorts, I was displaying kindness where many might have shot back in a rude or abrupt way. It is an extraordinary act that will blow his mind for some time. I know he thinks about this interaction, probably every time he sees Trump on TV! This man didn't necessarily deserve my kindness. Being the master communicator as well as a MCAW and knowing that I delight in furthering the cause of Conservatism and generating new thinking in the mind of man I had no other option than to extend to him a measure of kindness.

Now, had Mr. Wonderful been violent in his response I might have continued on in conversation setting up more boundaries and shifting the energy toward others in line, altering the path of interaction. I am so glad this was not the case and Conservatism won again.

There are many ways to display genuine and authentic kindness in communication. It will help nurture a conversation and bring healing. Showing mutual respect is also another way of showing kindles.

I: INTUITION

Follow your intuition when dealing with children, family, and church or community members, go with your gut. I know we discussed this earlier in the text. There can't be enough stress on the point of learning to trust yourself.

Your ability to adapt to the situation using all the skills and "TOOLS" you learned earlier is essential. By following your intuition, you may be able to avoid costly mistakes in communication with your closest relationships as well. Stay alert. Your "gut" will talk to you, if you listen!

M: MATURITY

Maturity or displays of maturity have been drastically reduced in the United States where communications is concerned. Frankly, we as women, as MCAWs should be leading by example, paving the way in this area and encouraging restoration. When you see something, say something. As leaders, as women, it is our duty to our families and our community circles to approach situations in a mature way, in a wholesome and becoming way and show future generations how the world ought to be operating. Much of the lack of civility we see today is because of a lack of inner maturity.

People are not just acting irresponsibly, they are in fact immature, and perhaps unequipped to communicate fully at the levels they should be according to their age. Be a leader, you will find that people will look up to and the conversations you have when you approach things in a mature manner, suddenly they almost become effortless. Also, as Women, MCAW you should be pressing for others to display their maturity. Call them on their shortcomings, in a mature way of course, displaying kindness.

Remember friends and family do not always tell us what we want to hear. Our friends and family are to be honest with us. Please encourage our younger generations in their communication to be mature and approach topics with the dignity and respect they deserve. Maturity is a sign of a well-balanced person. As a Modern Conservative American Woman, this should be you!

Chapter Fourteen

CONSCIENCE COMES HOME

As YOU CAN SEE, depending on the person, context and situation there are many different ways you can respond. Being a woman, and a MCAW to boot puts you at an advantage. Likely, you are in touch with your more sensitive and feminine side, you are balanced in your thoughts for the most part already. This will aid you in your exploration and perfecting of your "TOOL BOX!" I have confidence that with practice you will be victorious in your quest and master the skills needed to foster and grow the type of environmental climate that is needed for Revolution America to take place in your mind and life.

In time, your relationships will start to flourish, and manifest the sort of Conservative values you hold true to yourself. Those around you may not even notice what is happening, what they will notice is that they feel good when they are around you. This is good, because as they observe, even without noticing they also pick up skills and traits or even ask you questions that you can follow up with information. You may also be able to share how you came about your Revolution America experience and share with them how they can better their interactions with others, if they are open to it of course.

There have been countless people I have wanted to be able to hand this book to. When I talk to people, they become so open and pliable, even curious about how to better communicate. Even when someone has hated me for my views I have been able to get to the point in conversation where the topic is no longer about the conflict, rather the conversation shifts to how we can talk about things and get things done across party lines.

The guts and truth is that people want beautiful, happy relationships and interactions. It is that simple. Very few people want to live in constant conflict. I get that aunt or uncle in the family may be grumpy, but have you ever sat and really listened to them and their needs? The struggle of the Negative Aunt Nancys of the world may not even be noticed by even those closest to her, family members even. Try. Reach out.

We really should be looking to the good and right in people and to bettering lives. When we help the process and people feel better about their situations or about themselves we have put in opportunity for more conversations yet again.

It is essential we encourage this every chance we get! Our lives are a ministry, literally. To everyone we come in contact with. Our entire world is a space where we cannot only encourage good conversation, but we can direct and orchestrate through communication and conversation the changes in our families, in our communities or workspaces that will last lifetimes for generations to come.

We have to be led by conscience. There is little else that will guide you in your journey but your own desire and the drive your higher power or God has placed within you. Invest in what is pushing you to be your best in the relationships with the people around you.

Take from what your conscience is leading you to do and act on it. Many times we don't realize that we feel bad about a conversation, not because it was a bad conversation but because there is an inner pull somewhere in the interaction that is ushering us to look at what is really going on or taking place. Be open, entirely open to what this is. When this happens, close your eyes and think about the situation for a moment and tap into what is bothering you about what took place. Try to observe the negative, only to turn it into a power and positive way to approach resolution. When I think of Mr. Nice guy on isle 3, I knew in my gut I had to respond. This was a man who needed a lesson. Not a lesson as might be taught by a Liberal or Feminist, but one that would encourage positivity and provoke constructive thought. My conscience is loud. Had I passed up this opportunity in know I would have regretted it. So, I acted. You can too!

Remember failures and mistakes aren't bad if you learn from them. As you tune into what your purpose is and become more skilled in your means of communication there will be an ease of use that comes. A familiar voice from within will turn from a whisper to a loud voice you can trust. This comes in time.

There is a quiet and driving force that God or your higher power has put within you that will lead you, if only you tune in and listen to what it is saying. Your conscience can encourage you in many areas of your life if you are open to it. I believe that our Modern Conservative American Women mentioned earlier in the book were all driven by conscience. Conscience is consistent through your entire being, it is like a giant map. It is a moral compass of sorts. Follow it.

Chapter Fifteen

REVOLUTION AMERICA

IF YOU ARE TO BE Revolution America in your home, by the outward expression of what is in your mind you must reaffirm or restore personal and public confidence in your life path. This means that where there was conflict you should work toward healing, work toward fostering communication which encourages healing, accomplishing this may not be instant. Open dialog and healthy discourse must be a top priority for you, be confident and lead the way in the months and years to come.

As a leader in your circles you should display self-control, patience, understanding, and be of good moral standing. There should be a positive approach to communication even under the most complicated and difficult circumstances. It would be great to see a tough and challenging situation come your way and have your thoughts shift to positive, your emotions have a higher view of what is happening in the moment and your body response be that of moving on and taking care of the situation in a balanced way. This sort of shift from the original perspective in the book is what our outcome or goal should look like.

Dare to dream big about your ability to change your world. If you try, you might fail, but if you fail to try, you fail anyway. So act. Step out in confidence. Learn to challenge your thinking, observing your mind, your emotions, and actions. Repeat your lessons over and over until you master each area. Just by doing these things, there should be such a growth in your perception and understanding of your life, to the extent that the only true opinions which matter to you are that of yourself, your higher power or your God. Really, your personal view of yourself should trump all external sources. When you accomplish this, you will begin to operate in a space of fulfillment, and see yourself clear as day in your personal Revolution America.

Leading your home, showing others that your freedoms matter to you, and embracing the love that you have for yourself and extending it to others will pay dividends. You are the difference in this struggling world. You are the answer and solutions to problems and struggles in your home and community. Playing a large or small role is irrelevant, being involved and a present energy in your world is what matters, is what will realize the change in your space. Stay focused. And practice, practice, practice and put to work Your Personal Revolution America.

REFERENCES

(Endnotes)

1. "Discourse." *Merriam-Webster.com*. Merriam-Webster, n.d. Web. 16 Apr. 2017. *https://www.merriam-webster.com/dictionary/discourse*

2. "Dispute." *Merriam-Webster.com*. Merriam-Webster, n.d. Web. 16 Apr. 2017. *https://www.merriam-webster.com/dictionary/dispute*

3. "Debate." *Merriam-Webster.com*. Merriam-Webster, n.d. Web. 16 Apr. 2017. *https://www.merriam-webster.com/dictionary/debate*

4. "Woman." *Merriam-Webster.com*. Merriam-Webster, n.d. Web. 16 Apr. 2017. *https://www.merriam-webster.com/dictionary/woman*

5. "Womankind." *Merriam-Webster.com*. Merriam-Webster, n.d. Web. 16 Apr. 2017. *https://www.merriam-webster.com/dictionary/womankind*

6. "Tradition." *Merriam-Webster.com*. Merriam-Webster, n.d. Web. 8 May 2017. *https://www.merriam-webster.com/dictionary/tradition*

-- Traditional \-'dish-nəl, -'di-shə-n°l\ adjective

7. "Modern." *Merriam-Webster.com.* Merriam-Webster, n.d. Web. 8 May 2017. *https://www.merriam-webster.com/dictionary/modern*

8. "Feminism." *Merriam-Webster.com.* Merriam-Webster, n.d. Web. 8 May 2017. *https://www.merriam-webster.com/dictionary/feminism*
-- Feminist \'fe-mə-nist\ noun or adjective

9. "Conservative." *Merriam-Webster.com.* Merriam-Webster, n.d. Web. 8 May 2017. *https://www.merriam-webster.com/dictionary/conservative*

10. "Liberal." *Merriam-Webster.com.* Merriam-Webster, n.d. Web. 8 May 2017.

11. "American." *Merriam-Webster.com.* Merriam-Webster, n.d. Web. 10 May 2017.

12. *O'Brien, Mary Barmeyer (1995). Jeannette Rankin, 1880–1973 : bright star in the big sky. Helena, Mont.: Falcon Press. ISBN 1560442654.*

13. SOLAR: http://www.ocr.org.uk/Images/83070-unit-01-developing-effective-communication-in-health-and-social-care-teacher-instructions.pdf

14. SURETY: *stickley, "From SOLER to SURETY for effective non-verbal communication."* 2011 Nov;11(6):395-8. doi: 10.1016/j.nepr.2011.03.021. Epub 2011 Apr 13.

CPSIA information can be obtained
at www.ICGtesting.com
Printed in the USA
FSHW04n0529170418
46860FS

9 781628 654875